A SOCIO-DEMOGRAPHIC STUDY ON WOMAN AND CHILD HEALTH DIFFERENTIALS IN SLUMS OF KOLKATA

Madhumita Nath

Acknowledgement

It is a great opportunity for me to express gratitude to all the people who have helped and encouraged me in various ways in carrying out this study.

My deepest gratitude goes to **all the respondents** of this study mainly the household helps, maids and their children for their voluntary participation ,providing data on different occasions , taking out time out of their schedule , constant encouragement and cooperation to pursue this work ,sometimes even if they are hungry and empty stomached .

It is my great honour to express my indebtedness to my supervisor **Professor Manibrata Bhattacharya**. I have been amazingly fortunate to have such an advisor who gave me the freedom to explore on my own and at the same time the guidance to recover when my steps faltered. He taught me how to question thoughts and express ideas. His patience and support helped me overcome many crisis situations and finish this thesis.

I am also grateful to late **Prof. (Dr.) Bela Bhattacharya** for her encouragement and practical advice. I am thankful to her for reading my reports; commenting on my views and helping me understand and enrich my ideas.

I owe profound debts to all **the Professors** of the **Department of Anthropology, Calcutta University** for their valuable suggestions and constructive criticisms at different stages of my research. I am also thankful to my **friends** and **seniors** in the **Anthropology Department, CU**, for their comments and academic discussions which was helpful in writing this dissertation.

I would like to convey my sincere thanks and gratitude to **Dr. Mitchell .G. Weiss** (Professor and Head, Dept. of Cultural Epidemiology, Swiss Tropical and Public Health Institute) , Ms. **Sandhya Diwakar** (ICMR, New Delhi) , Ms. **Jhilam Bannerjee** (Dept. of Psychiatric Social Work ,Institute of Psychiatry ,Kolkata) , **Dr. Md. Shah Noorur Rahman** (North-East Hill University, Shillong) and **Dr. Rimai Joy** (Dept. of Anthropology, Amity University) for their discussions on related topics and valuable advices that helped me improve my knowledge in the area.

I appreciate the financial support from the Indian Council of Medical Research (ICMR), New Delhi that funded parts of this research project.

I am also grateful to the **staffs** of the Anthropology Department, **University of Calcutta** for their various forms of support during my study.

Last but not the least; I am immensely grateful to **my parents.** None of this would have been possible without their love and patience; my mother who emphasized the importance of education, my father who has been my role-model for hard work, persistence and personal sacrifices, and **my little son** who is not only a constant source of love, concern and strength but is also the motivation for this work. I must also acknowledge the role of my husband without whose love, encouragement and editing assistance this work would never have been completed.

Madhumita Nath

TABLE OF CONTENTS   Page No.

Acknowledgment		i
List of Tables		vi
List of Figures		x
Chapter 1	**Introduction**	1
1.1	Trends of Urbanization	2
1.2	The slums of Kolkata	4
1.3	Objectives of the present study	9
1.4	Scope of the Study	10
1.5	Materials and Methods	11
1.6	Study design	12
1.7	Research Strategy	16
1.8	Preparation of schedules and questionnaires	17
1.9	Data Types	17
1.10	Ethical considerations	20
1.11	Overview of the thesis	21
Chapter 2	**Kolkata city and Slums**	22
2.1	Kolkata – a brief history	23
2.2	Religion	25
2.3	Kolkata Slums	25
2.4	Slums - meaning and types	27
2.5	Physical structure of housing in slums	29
2.6	Attributes of Slums	31
2.7	Socio-economic and Household Characteristics of the Kolkata slums	32
2.7.1	Solid Waste Disposal	33

			Page No.
	2.7.2	Drainage	34
	2.7.3	Number of rooms	35
	2.7.4	Ventilation	37
	2.7.5	Lighting	39
	2.7.6	Drinking water	41
	2.7.7	Sanitation	43
	2.8	Household expenditure	47
Chapter 3		**The Slum Women and Children**	50
	3.1	Demographic profile of the sample population	50
	3.2	Age structure of the female population	53
	3.3.	Age–sex structure of the child population	54
	3.4	Marital Status	55
	3.5	Educational Standard	57
	3.6	Occupational pursuits	60
	3.7	Income	63
	3.8	Travelling Time to work	67
	3.9	Means of commute	68
Chapter 4		**Reproductive Health Behaviour**	70
	4.1	Age of menarche	70
	4.2	Age at First marriage	72
	4.3	Age of Mothers at First Child Birth	73
	4.4	Age of women at their Last Child Birth	74
	4.5	Number of Children Ever-born and Living	75
	4.6	Reproductive health	77

			Page No.
	4.7	Self reported symptoms of gynecological problems	77
	4.7.1	Duration of the Symptoms	78
	4.8	Child care	79
Chapter 5		**Women's health in slums**	82
	5.1	Family planning: Use of contraceptives	82
	5.2	Maternal Health Care	85
	5.2.1	Antenatal Care (ANC)	86
	5.3	Place of Delivery	88
	5.4	Awareness about AIDS	92
	5.4.1	AIDS awareness among the studied population:	96
	5.4.2	'Safe' and 'Risky' behaviors	98
	5.5	Alternative healthcare	100
Chapter 6		**Child Health and Diseases in Slums**	105
	6.1	Child Immunization	105
	6.2	Childhood Diseases	109
	6.3	Child Morbidity and Treatment	112
	6.4	Breastfeeding practices	119
Chapter 7		**Determinants of fertility, infant mortality**	123
Chapter 8		**Summary and observations**	135
		References	148
		Appendix	162

LIST OF TABLES
Page No.

1.1	Statistical Profile of West Bengal and India (2011 Census)	3
1.2	Population of West Bengal by sex and residence: 2011	3
1.3	Population of India by sex and residence: 2011	4
1.4	Tabular representation of the name and address of the studied slums	14
2.1	Demographic Profile of Kolkata	22
2.2	Population of Kolkata by different religious beliefs	25
2.3	Total Population and Slum Population of Kolkata by sex.	26
2.4	Frequency and percentage distribution of garbage removal	34
2.5	Drainage facilities in the slum areas	34
2.6	Frequency and percentage distribution of number of rooms	36
2.7	Frequency and percentage distribution of presence of windows	38
2.8	Frequency and percentage distribution of number of windows and ventilators	38
2.9	Frequency and percentage distribution of source of lighting	39
2.10	Frequency and percentage distribution of source of water	41
2.11	Availability of Bathing Facility	43
2.12	Availability of Latrine Facility in slum households	46
2.13	Expenditure pattern of Kolkata slum households	48
3.1	Age-sex structure of the total population with age-specific sex ratios	51
3.2	Age structure of the studied female population	53
3.3	Age-sex distribution of the child population	54
3.4	Distribution of marital status of female population	56
3.5	Educational status of the studied population	57
3.6	Educational status of the female population by age groups and the standard of education	59

		Page No.
3.7	Occupational pursuits of the studied female population	60
3.8	Frequency distribution of the working hours of the respondents	62
3.9	Income per month generated by the studied women	64
3.10	Time Taken to Travel at work place by the women	67
3.11	Frequency and percentage distribution of means of commutation	68
4.1	Frequency and percentage distribution of age of menarche among women	71
4.2	Frequency and percentage distribution of age of women at their first marriage	72
4.3	Percent distribution of ever married women aged 15-49 years, by age at first childbirth and present age	74
4.4	Percent distribution of ever married women by age at last childbirth and present age	74
4.5	Percent distribution of ever-married women aged 15-49 years, by number of children ever born and mean number of children ever born and living	75
4.6	Percentage of women reporting current symptoms associated with gynecological morbidity, and percentage distribution of duration of specific symptoms	78
4.7	Percent distribution of individuals taking care of the child during mother's illness	80
5.1	Frequency and percentage of women adopting various methods of family planning through contraceptives	82
5.2	Frequency and percentage distribution of women using different methods of family planning	83
5.3	Frequency and percentage distribution of various reasons for not adopting birth control measures	84
5.4	Frequency and distribution of home visits made by health or family planning workers in these slums	85
5.5	Percentage of live births (during the four-year period prior to the study), by whether the mother received antenatal check-ups	87

		Page No.
5.6	Percentage of live births (during the four-year period prior to the study), by number of antenatal checkup visits and, by the stage of pregnancy at the time of first visit	87
5.7	Distribution of live births (during the four-year period prior to the study), by mother's education and place of delivery	88
5.8	Distribution of live births (during the four-year period prior to the study), By place of delivery and mother's age at birth of first child	89
5.9	Distribution of live births (during the four-year period prior to the study), by place of delivery and Birth Order	90
5.10	Distribution of live births (during the four-year period prior to the study), by place of delivery and Antenatal Care (ANC) received	90
5.11	Frequency and percentage of respondents visiting public hospitals	91
5.12	Frequency and percentage distribution of women having prior information about menstruation and childbirth	92
5.13	Frequency and percentage distribution of source of information about menstruation, AIDS, among these women.	93
5.14	Frequency and percentage distribution of women's reaction on the initial onset of menstruation and news of pregnancy	94
5.15	Frequency and percentage distribution of women agreeing/ disagreeing to rituals performed after attending menarche, pregnancy	95
5.16	Frequency and percentage distribution of women continuing their work during illness and pregnancy	95
5.17	Frequency and percentage of women having knowledge of AIDS	96
5.18	Frequency and percentage distribution of women believing in different ways of prevention of AIDS	97
5.19	Frequency and percentage distribution of women's perception of 'safe' behaviors	98
5.20	Frequency and percentage distribution of women's perception of 'risky' behaviors	99
5.21	Frequency and percentage distribution of women taking alternative medical treatment in the last five years	101

		Page No.
5.22	Frequency and percentage distribution of women citing various reasons for taking alternative medical treatment in the last five years	102
5.23	Frequency and percentage distribution of different types of alternative medical treatments	103
6.1	Distribution of child population immunized in the slum	106
6.2	Frequency Distribution of infants and children (aged between 0-4 years) suffering from various diseases	110
6.3	Distribution of children under four years of age, having common ailments like cough, fever, and diarrhea	112
6.4	Percent distribution of children under four years of age, having cough, by treatment	114
6.5	Percent distribution of children under four years of age having fever, flu in the past two weeks, by treatment	115
6.6	Percent distribution of children less than four years of age, having diarrhea in the past two weeks, by whether treated or not; sex of the child and mother's education	116
6.7	Percent distribution of children having diarrhoea in the past two weeks, by age and feeding practices during diarrhoea	117
6.8	Distribution of children under four years of age according to present breastfeeding status by age and sex of the children	119
6.9	Percent distribution of duration (in months) of children breast fed by their mother	120
7.1	Correlation results of Hypothesis 1	124
7.2	Model summary of different factors establishing alternative Hypothesis 1	126
7.3	Correlation of Hypothesis 2	128
7.4	Model summary of factors establishing alternative Hypothesis 2	129
7.5	Correlation of Hypothesis 3	131
7.6	Model summary of different factors establishing alternative Hypothesis 3	133

LIST OF FIGURES   **Page No.**

1	Map of the Kolkata Metropolitan Area	13
2	Map showing the different wards under study of Kolkata Municipal Corporation (highlighted areas)	15
3	Schematic Framework for the study	20
4	Map Showing Percentage of Slum Population to Total Population in different wards of Kolkata Municipal Corporation.	26
5	A view of Kolkata slum	28
6	A ' Semi pucca' house in slum with bamboo-thatched roof and brick wall	29
7	A club in the slum-area	30
8	The entrance to the studied slum-area	30
9	'Semi -pucca' dwelling hut in slum	31
10	Garbage removal in slum	33
11	A child in Slum house	35
12	Slum lane	35
13	Graphical representation of number of rooms of each slum household	36
14	Slum house ventilation	37
15	Graphical representation of the presence of windows/ventilators in slums	39

		Page No.
16	Graphical representation of the source of lighting in the slum households	40
17	A slum household with electricity	40
18	Source of potable water in slum	42
19	A child drinking water from its source	42
20	Open bathing space in slum house	43
21	A girl washing clothes in slum house	44
22	Availability of bathing Facility within slum premises	44
23	Toilet facility inside house in slum	45
24	An open urinal in slum	45
25	The availability of Latrine Facility in slums of Kolkata	47
26	Graphical Representation of the Expenditure pattern in Kolkata slums	48
27	A slum family	49
28	Graphical representation of the total slum population by different age groups	52
29	Distribution of the studied female population by different age groups.	53
30	A slum woman with her child	55
31	Graphical representation of the marital status of the studied population.	56
32	Graphical representation of the educational status of the studied population.	57
33	Slum girls in front of school	58
34	"Zari " workers in slum	58

		Page No.
35	Graphical representation of different types of occupational categories of the women	61
36	A women cooking in her slum house-cum-shop.	52
37	Graphical representation (in percentage) of total working hours by women in slums	63
38	Graphical representation (in percentage) of monthly income	64
39	Household utensils	65
40	Clothes and utensils in a slum household	65
41	A slum room	66
42	A slum woman in bedroom-cum-kitchen	66
43	Graphical representation of total time taken to commute by the respondent	67
44	Graphical representation of the various means to commute	69
45	Graphical representation of age of menarche among women	71
46	Graphical representation of age of women at their first marriage	72
47	Married female respondents at the Chetla slum	73
48	Children living in the slum	76
49	Graphical representation of the number of children ever born to women	77
50	A slum women suffering from fistula	79
51	Mother with her two children	81
52	Graphical representation of women using contraceptives for family planning	83
53	Graphical representation of different methods of family planning practices	84

		Page No.
54	Graphical representation of various reasons owing to which women ignore birth control measures.	85
55	Graphical representation of home visits made by health or family planning workers	86
56	Percentage of live births.	89
57	Graphical representation of respondent's visit to any public hospitals	91
58	Graphical representation of women having prior information about menstruation and childbirth	92
59	Graphical representation of source of information about menstruation, AIDS, among these women	93
60	Graphical representation of women's reaction on the initial onset of menstruation and news of pregnancy	94
61	Graphical representation of women continuing their work during illness and pregnancy	96
62	Graphical representation of AIDS awareness among women	97
63	Graphical representation of women believing in different ways of prevention of AIDS	98
64	Graphical representation of women's perception of 'safe' behaviors	99
65	Graphical representation of women's perception of 'risky' behaviors	100
66	Graphical representation of women taking alternative medical treatment in the last five years	101

		Page No.
67	Graphical representation of women taking alternative medical treatment in the last five years	102
68	Graphical representation of alternative medical treatments used by women in the study population	104
69	Children in the slum	107
70	A child recently immunised	107
71	Reasons for not vaccinating	109
72	Graphical representation of children and infants (aged between 0-4 years) suffering from disease in past one year	110
73	Graphical representation of nature of disease among children	111
74	Graphical representation of places of treatment of children	113
75	Children working in a shop	113
76	A polyclinic in the slum area	114
77	A child in the slum house	118
78	A Breastfed baby girl	121
79	Graphical representation of duration of children breast fed (in months)	122

Chapter 1

Introduction

Urbanization is an important social phenomenon that involves an array of interrelated process of demographic, economic, environmental and technological changes. The twentieth century witnessed a rapid urbanisation of the world's population. The global proportion of urban population increased from a mere 13 per cent in 1900 to 29 per cent in 1950 and, reached 49 per cent in 2005. The rising numbers of urban dwellers give the best indication of the scale of these unprecedented trends: the urban population increased from 220 million in 1900 to 732 million in 1950, and reached 3.2 billion in 2005, thus more than quadrupling since 1950. In the middle of the year 2009, the number of people living in urban areas (3.42 billion) surpassed the number living in rural areas (3.41 billion), thus more than quadrupling since 1950. Since then the world has become more urban than rural. 'Urban' refers to an area where a multiplicity of communities of substantial size (minimum population of 5,000) and density (at least 400 people per sq km) live with a variety of non-agricultural pursuits, with good infrastructure facilities. However, this urban expansion is not a phenomenon of wealthy countries. Major part of the growth has occurred in unplanned and under-served city slums. The pace of urbanization exceeds the rate at which basic infrastructure and services can be provided, and the consequences for the urban poor have been dire. At present more than 32 percent of the world's urban population are estimated to live in slums. Failure to prepare for this unprecedented and inevitable urban explosion carries serious implications for global security and environmental sustainability. Therefore, this is noteworthy in demographic history that though more than fifty percent of world's population live in urban areas yet one third of them are in a state of chronic poverty. One billion people which is almost one-third of the world's urban population, currently live in slums. The absolute number of urban poor has increased in the last fifteen to twenty years at a rate faster than that in rural areas. Global poverty has become an urban phenomenon. In the year 2002, 746 million people in urban areas were living on less than $2.00 a day (Ravallion 2007, 16). Rapid urban growth has made Asia home to the largest share of the world's slum dwellers. Therefore, though urbanization is an important and positive transformation, linked to economic growth and a better educated and productive labour force; it could also contribute to greater environmental sustainability, and to improved social welfare through better access to services. But this can only be achieved by policies and planning that use a gendered perspective to look at various aspects of urban poverty that stretches beyond income, to include domestic and care responsibilities, dependency and health of women.

1.1 Trends of Urbanization in India, West Bengal and Kolkata

India as the rest of the world also is getting urbanized. Rate of urbanization in India has increased from 27.81% in 2001 Census to 31.16% in 2011 Census. The urban population of India is one of the largest in the world at 377.1 million inhabitants, equivalent of almost the entire population of the United States of America.

West Bengal is the fourth most populated state in India with one of the most population density. The state has a population of about 91.3 million according to 2011 census. In fact, it is considered as the ninth most populated state in the world. The overall growth rate of population of the state is about 14% which is below the national average, whereas the growth in urban population is about 30% which is nearly the same as the national average. The population density is 1028, much higher when compared to the national average of 382. The state sex ratio stands at 950. Literacy rate is 76%, marginally above nationl avarage of 74%. A demographic profile of West Bengal and India based on 2011 census is given below.

Table 1.1   Statistical Profile of West Bengal and India (2011 Census)

	West Bengal	India
Total Population (in millions)	91.3	1210.2
Urban Population (in millions)	29.1	377.1
Percentage of urban to total population	31.87	31.16
Decadal Population Growth (percentage)	13.84	17.64
Decadal Urban Population Growth (percentage)	29.72	31.8
Population Density (per sq. km.)	1028	382
Sex ratio (females per 1000 males)	950	940
Child Sex ratio(0-6)	956	914
Literacy (percentage)	76.3	74.4

Some Basic Statistics of Urban Population in West Bengal and India are given in Table 1.2 and Table 1.3.

Table 1.2 Population of West Bengal by sex and residence: as per Census 2011

Table 1.2	Population of West Bengal by sex and residence: 2011			
India	Male	Female	Total population	Sex ratio
Urban	14,964,082	14,128,920	29,093,002	944
Rural	31,844,945	30,338,168	62,183,113	953
Total	46,809,027	44,467,088	91,276,115	950

Table 1.3	Population of India by sex and residence: 2011			
India	Male	Female	Total population	Sex ratio
Urban	19,58,07,196	18,12,98,564	37,71,05,760	926
Rural	42,79,17,052	40,51,70,610	83,30,87,662	947
Total	62,37,24,248	58,64,69,174	1,21,01,93,422	940

The total number of urban dwellers in West Bengal as per the population total, of the census of India, 2011 is 29,093,002. The total number of urban dwellers in the country is 37, 71, 05,760. The percentage of urban population to the total population in the country works out to 31.16% as against 31.87% in West Bengal.

The Census of India 2011 suggests that 66% of all statutory towns in India have slums where 17.4% of total urban households currently resides. Urban poverty and slum growth are local problems, but their nature and scale demand a global response.

Kolkata is the capital city of West Bengal. Kolkata Municipal Corporation has a population of 4580544 as of 2011 Census, with a poplulation density of 24,430 per square kilometer. It is one of the megacities in India and also one of the largest urban agglomerations in the world. However the process of urbanization and the unprecedented growth in the urban population has resulted in acute housing deficit and increasing poverty. Thereby compelling the poor population of the city to reside in the slums.

1.2 The slums of Kolkata

The slums of Kolkata are probably as old as the city itself. They can be divided into three groups: the older ones, up to 150 years' old, in the heart of the city, are associated with early urbanization. The second group dates from the 1940s and 1950s and emerged as an outcome of industrialization-based rural–urban migration, locating themselves around industrial sites and near infra-structural arteries. The third group came into being after the independence of India and took vacant urban lands and areas along roads, canals and on marginal lands. In 2001, 1.5 million people, or one third of Kolkata's population, lived in more than five thousand five hundred slums of which 2011 are registered and 3500 unregistered slums. Slums of Kolkata are often characterized by deteriorating or poorly structured houses crowded together, poor environmental managements such as deficient access to safe drinking water and sanitation, stagnation of water and poor drainage with excessive open sewers, excessive amount of uncollected rubbish, severe over-crowding, flies, and poor lighting and ventilation which affect the health of the slum-dwellers in various ways.

The slums of Kolkata have often been conceptualized as social clusters that engender a distinct set of health problems and depict the worst health conditions. The poor environmental condition coupled with high population density makes them a major reservoir for a wide spectrum of adverse health conditions such as undernutrition, delivery–related complications, postpartum morbidity (Mony et.al, 2006). Brilliant films have been made by Satyajit Ray, Ritwik Ghatak, Mrinal Sen, who have documented the internal motif and the material conditions of the life and living of the 'unfortunate' women of Kolkata slums. Different Indian and foreign scholars have also made systematic and critical studies on slums. However, there have been limited efforts to study the health of individuals specially women living in slums. Of the few studies that exist, Mahadevan (1979) had attempted to discover the socio-cultural factors responsible for the differences in fertility behaviour in his micro-level study of different castes of Madurai district in Tamil Nadu. Later he along with Chandrasekaran, Freedman and others (1982) provided an understanding of the socio-economic determinants of fertility, mortality, and demographic transition along with a conceptual model on health and mortality. Earlier Davis Kingsley (1951) had noted the general inverse relationship between caste-status and fertility. Till then, very few micro-level studies were undertaken to explore the how and why of this interesting proposition. Later studies of Agarwala (1970) and Wyon & Gordon (1971), however do not support this hypothesis. Bhargava (1991) gave an overview of the current status of Neonatal Care and alternative strategies for reduction of neonatal mortality in the decade of nineties. McCarthy and Deborah (1992) provided the framework for analyzing the determinants of maternal mortality. Osmani (1992) addressed issues arising from poverty in terms of nutritional status, the role of anthropometry and gender bias in allocation of nutrients and health care. Prakash (1993) in her article suggested some new approaches to Women's Health Care. Chatterjee (1993) made her study on the health conditions of the poor masses of India. Roy Bardhan (1994) studied the slums of Kolkata and made a retrospective study of the public policies. Sen and Dreze (1995) pointed out the insufficient and ineffective activity of the Indian Government in the field of health care and social security. Cassels (1995), in his discussion paper gave an overview on the key issues of health sector reforms in less developed countries. Bhattacharya (1996) studied the salient socio-demographic features of the slums and pavement dwellers of Kolkata metropolis. Mitra and others (1998) concentrated on the health aspects of the slum dwellers in Delhi and described them as an 'unhealthy population'. The 52nd Round of National Sample Survey Organisation (1998) indicated that the poor are forced to spend a disproportionately higher percentage (12%) of their income on health services and nearly a fifth do not avail treatment at all. National Family Health Survey-2 (1998-99) points out that despite nationwide programme for nutritional supplementation for pregnant woman and children, available indicators present a pessimistic scenario. Bos, Hon, Akiko and Chellaraj (1999) made a statistical analysis of the health, nutrition and population indicators. Gupta and Baghel (1999) in their study on Indian slums attempted to elucidate and explain the levels, differentials, causes and determinants of infant mortality in Calcutta Metropolis and Raipur City (M.P.). The infant mortality rate (IMR) in the slums was found to be quite high but lower than that in rural India, underlining the importance of urban residence as a major controlling factor of infant mortality. The IMR in the slums of Calcutta was about one and a half times that in the slums of Raipur, suggesting that slum infant mortality is far worse in metropolises than in smaller cities. A number of individual-level, household-level and slum-level determinants were examined, and all played some explanatory role, but the differences in neighbourhood environment contributed most substantially to the infant mortality differential between the slums of Calcutta and Raipur. Claeson and Pathmanathan (1999) suggested some ways of reducing child mortality in India. Balasubramanian (2000) studied the issues and strategies for the improvement of maternal survival in India. Das and Coutinho (2000) in their article made a sociological enquiry with regard to disease control and immunization. Feachem and Gwatkin (2000) focused on inequalities in health and identified poverty, literacy, fertility and nutrition as the key areas influencing health outcomes. Loudon (2000) had observed the incidence of maternal mortality in the past and established the relevance of her study in the developing countries. Rush (2000) in his paper studied the inter-linkage between nutrition and maternal mortality. Ramachandran and others (2001) reviewed the progress of the 'Health, Nutrition and Family Welfare Programme' during the Ninth Plan Period. Qadeer, Sen and Nayar (2001) highlighted the political economy of Public Health in South Asia and gave critical assessment on the health reforms. Bhattacharya and Bhattacharya (2003) gave an overview on some demographic characteristics of the slums of West Bengal at the beginning of Third Millennium. Mishra, Chatterjee and Rao (2003) provided the vital statistics on current health scenario of India and gave an overview on the State's role in health, HIV/AIDS, public and private health care, drug policy and regulations and the potential of health research in India. The UN-Habitat Global Report on Human Settlements (2003) provided an understanding of the challenges of the slums. Infant mortality rate in the slums is a reliable indicator of health status and well-being of the children. Besides, it reflects the socioeconomic development of the population. The study of infant mortality is significant, especially because mortality during the first year of life is invariably high for all countries, irrespective of whether the overall levels of mortality are high or low. Infant and child mortality is relatively higher in groups where fertility is higher, i.e., increased mortality is response to high fertility (Chen et al., 1974; Choudhury et al., 1976).Another relationship is also well recognized i.e., high fertility is a biological and behavioural response to high mortality (Preston, 1978). In single terms higher infant mortality tends to higher fertility and vice-a-versa. Like fertility, infant mortality is also influenced by a number of factors such as parent's education particularly that of mother (Caldwell, 1979; Nag, 1983; Bhasin and Kshatriya, 1990; UN, 1994) and access to medical facilities (UN, 1985; Jain, 1985; Mahadevan, 1989; Suri Babu and Bhasin, 1990; Chachra and Bhasin, 1998c; Bhasin and Nag, 2002). In India, mother's education (individual level variable), income (household level variable), and availability of medical facilities and care (community level variable), are major determinants of infant and child mortality (Jain, 1985). Closely related to fertility is birth control. Birth control in its modern application means the conscious responsible control of conception (Unger, 2013). Family planning through contraception aims to achieve two main objectives; firstly to have only the desired number of children and secondly to have these children by proper spacing of pregnancies. In India, there has been a considerable increase in the governmental and non-governmental activities for promoting the adoption of family planning through widespread and intensified efforts as well as clinical services being made available to the users of family planning methods. Acceptance of contraception by a couple is governed by various socio-cultural factors, such as religion (NFHS: 1998-99, 2002) and education of husband and wife (Coale, 1965; Berelson, 1976). In India, the states with greater contraceptive use have generally achieved a more advanced state of socioeconomic modernization. Mass media plays an important role in promotion and acceptability of contraception (Bhat, 1996; Ramesh et al., 1996). Spousal communication also increases the likelihood of contraceptive use (Lasee and Becker, 1997; Kamal, 1999; Ghosh, 2001). In addition to this, religious affiliation affects the acceptance of sterilization due to behaviour related to childbearing (Chacko, 1988; Goldscheider and Mosher, 1988; Reddy, 1996). Contraceptive prevalence rate is found to be lower among the Muslim and lower caste Hindu women (Gulati, 1996; Bora et al., 1998). Rajani and Dua (2005) in their review of women and children's health in India focused on safe mother hood and the burden of disease. Agarwal and Taneja (2005) discussed a number of factors that could increase health vulnerability among the urban poor. Government of India (2011) took an attempt to review the trend of urban poverty from 1951 to 2011 in India and evaluate the existing programme for the improvement of urban poor. However, the major limitation of most of these studies is that they have been either confined to a specific area or cities, or the findings have totally been generalized. It is also evident that micro-level social studies about reproductive morbidity and its determinants in Indian slums are almost nonexistent. In view of these, the objectives of the present study are as follows:

1.3 Objectives of the present study

The main objectives of the study based on the Kolkata slums are:

- To assess the health of the individuals, specially women and children, living in different slums of Kolkata

- To ascertain the socio-demographic determinants influencing the health conditions of women population engaged in various occupations living in the slums

- To review the impact of the environmental and housing conditions on the health of women and children

- To ascertain how different socio-economic and cultural factors play crucial role in determining the fertility, family planning, acceptance of contraceptives and overall health of the mother and child.

- To evaluate the availability and utilization pattern of the reproductive and child health services in the slums.

1.4 Scope of the Study

This study looks at different aspects of poverty that impacts negatively both women and children's health. The women living here have very little opportunity to have decent lifestyles in spite of having immense responsibilities towards their family. The factors such as poverty, overwork and social inequality are accounted for considerable neglect of their health. The demands of managing a house, taking care of the husband and children and going out to work to bring in extra money tends to place the women's own health quite low on the list of priorities .It may be often seen that unless they have more than one complaint of ill health they do not seek medical treatment. A number of socioeconomic and cultural factors (distant determinants) operate through a set of intermediate determinants (health status, reproductive status, access to health services, extent of utilization of health services) to determine the level of maternal and child well-being. Unlike rural areas, which have a dedicated government health care structure, urban areas do not have such a structure. Further medical costs, timings, distance and other factors put the secondary care and private sector facilities out of reach of most urban poor .Therefore concerted efforts are needed to offer useful data to the health planners as well as policymakers in order to get relevant strategies that could be designed for bringing improvements in health conditions of this disadvantaged population. Methodology plays a crucial part in social studies, without which results are likely to be unreliable and defective. For the present study a descriptive research design based on the qualitative and quantitative data was taken up to determine the socio-demographic conditions that determine the health status of the women and children in the slums of Kolkata. The nature of the study is unconventional and multidisciplinary, concentrating on the systematic understanding of the health conditions of the women and children. The present work also attempts to identify the sociodemographic factors that influence the utilization of the reproductive health services among women in the slums.

1.5 Materials and Methods

The key methods that have been used in this study for collecting the data are:

a. Anthropological methods that include case study method, participant observation method along social surveys with open-ended questionnaires and schedules.

b. Statistical designs adopting the multi-stage stratified and random sampling.

c. Besides, health conditions were accessed through health survey in order to collect data on individual health problems and/or ailment symptoms affecting the individual.

The data were collected by repeated visits to the selected households by the researcher herself. The questionnaires administered during the field work covered topics including antenatal, delivery, postnatal care, reproductive history, contraceptive use, etc. Later on analysis of data was done with the help of Statistical Package for Social Science. The relation among the key sociodemographic variables are described using distribution frequencies of the data. Further analysis was done by using the multivariate logistic regression. This was done to identify factors that are associated with the use of the reproductive health services, namely, use of modern contraceptive methods; availing antenatal services defined as at least three ANC visits; use of skilled birth attendants; and place of delivery.

1.6 Study design :

In this present study four slums within the Kolkata Municipal Area were randomly taken up. It was convenient to conduct intensive fieldwork in and around these areas as there are large concentrations of woman and child population are residing in these slum areas. 559 ever-married women of the reproductive age groups were selected from 559 households from four different slums located one each in Ward No –78 (Borough-IX) and Ward No-86 (Borough-VIII) respectively and two slums located in Ward no-82 (Borough –IX) were taken up. The fieldwork was done in several installments over a quite long time period because it was necessary to establish good rapport with the subjects of the study in order to get good quality data. The communication with the subjects was renewed through frequent visits to their households in the slums for data collection.

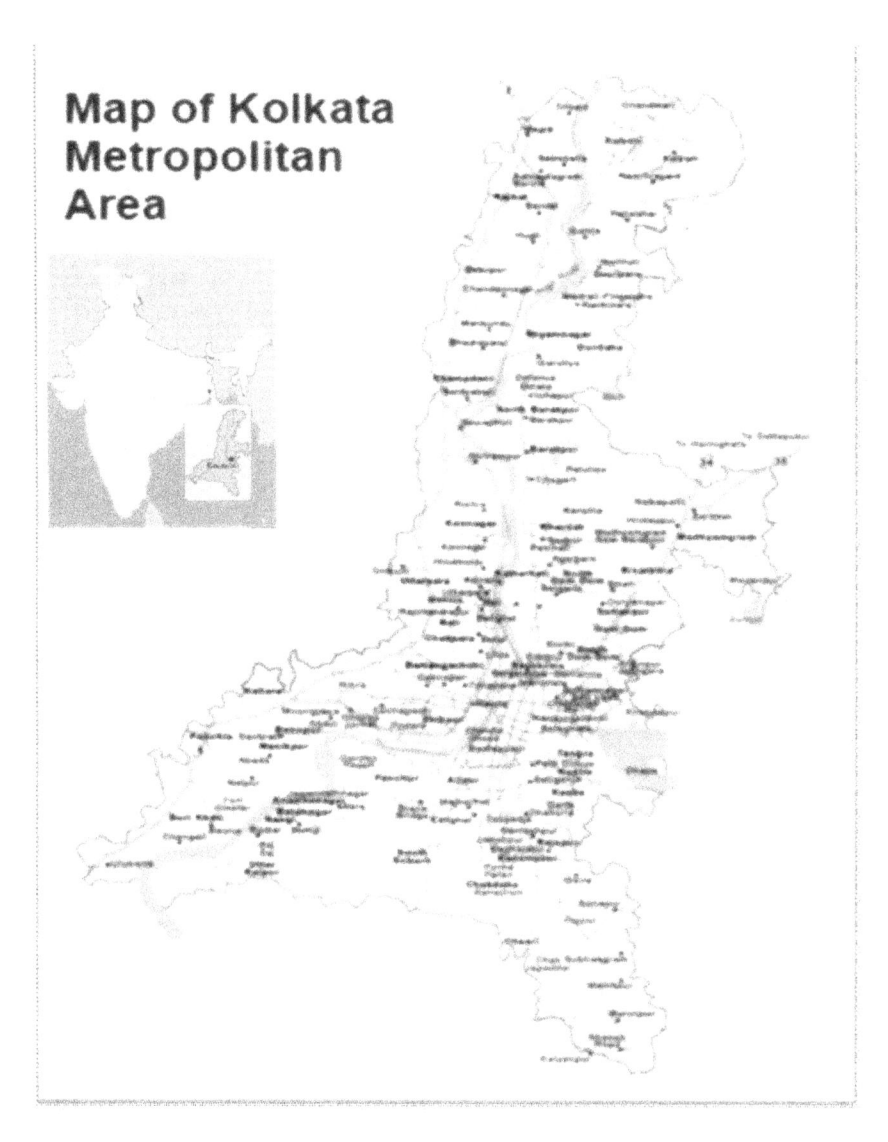

Figure 1: Map of the Kolkata Metropolitan Area
(Source: Kolkata Municipal Corporation, 2011)

Table 1.4. Tabular representation of the name and address of the studied slums[1]

Sl. No.	Ward No.	Borough Number	Addresses of the studied Slums	No. of studied households	Percentage
1	78	IX	19/A Chetla Haat road, Kolkata- 700027	114	20.39
2	82	IX	42, Ekbalpur lane, Kolkata-700023	108	19.32
3	82	IX	50, Diamond Harbour road, Kolkata-23	135	24.15
4	86	VIII	41/3 Chetla Road, Kolkata -700029	202	36.14
	Total			**559**	**100.00**

---

[1]*The Kolkata city is divided into 144 administrative wards that are grouped into 15 boroughs. Each of these wards elects a councillor to the Kolkata Municipal Corporation or KMC. Each borough has a committee consisting of the councillors elected from the respective wards of the borough. The Corporation, through the borough committees, maintains government-aided schools, hospitals and municipal markets and partakes in urban planning and road maintenance.*

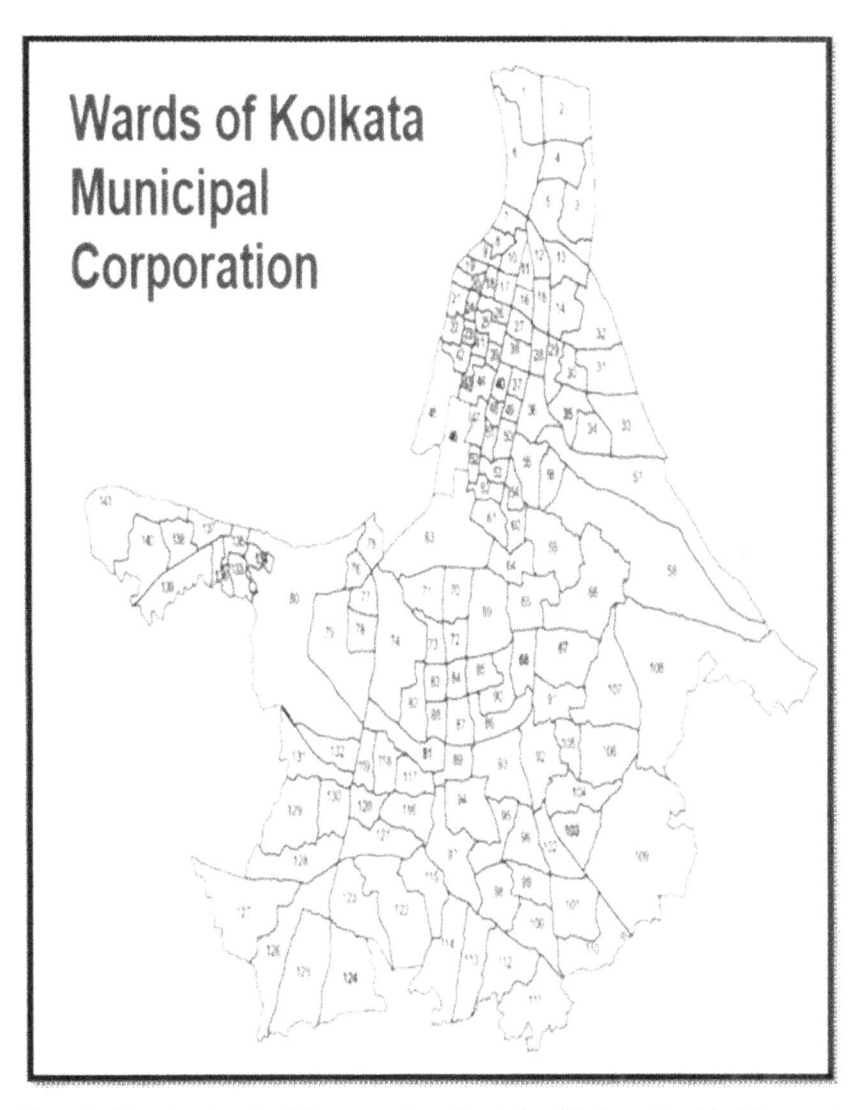

Figure 2: Map showing the different wards under study of Kolkata Municipal Corporation (highlighted areas)

Source: Kolkata Municipal Corporation, 2011

1.7 Research Strategy

The data have been collected in different phases of field work during 2009 to 2014 the details of which are mentioned below :

1. The first set of data was collected on the key social and demographic variables from 559 households from the ever-married women respondents who are between 15-49 years of age groups

2. Data on the second domain of interest was knowledge and current use of contraceptive methods among those women in the four selected slums located in various wards of Kolkata Municipal Corporation.

3. Data on the third domain was collected on antenatal care of selected sample female population. These data were collected in terms of frequency (number of visits), timing (in which trimester of pregnancy) and place of ANC services.

4. Data on the fourth domain of the study was collected on the place of delivery and postpartum care /check-up received by ever married and sampled female population and the health conditions of their children between 0-4 years of age groups. In this study an attempt has been made to study the effects related to different factors in infant mortality, fertility, as well as use of methods for controlling birth among the Kolkata slum dwellers. Its main aim is to identify the singular and collective relation among the variables that have impacted. The dependent variables considered in this study are fertility, infant mortality, and the use of birth control methods .The different independent variables considered are, women's age at present, women's age at marriage, age at menarche, number of live births per married women, ideal number of children, desired number of sons ,women's level of education, and income.

1.8 Preparation of schedules and questionnaires

Schedules were prepared and tested on the demography, women reproductive performance including fertility, morbidity, menarcheal and menopausal age, common aliment symptoms, activity pattern, health maintenance, educational and occupational status, child birth and antenatal care, child morbidity and treatment, feeding practices and supplementation methods prevalent among the studied population. Making repeat visits to the household rectified discrepancies. The completed questionnaires were again checked and edited before they were coded and processed by using SPSS software. Most of the interview was devoted to identify pathways by which the mother's education influences the health and survival of her child. Questions concerning respondents' reported symptoms of reproductive problems formed one of the 14 sections in the questionnaire. To compose the questions, a comprehensive list of reproductive morbidities (both obstetric and gynecological), including complete details of symptoms for each condition was prepared in everyday language that the women being interviewed could understand. This list was thoroughly pretested and translated into Bengali, the local language. The interview lasted for about two hours, of which about 20 minutes were devoted to the section on symptoms of reproductive morbidity and its treatment. The questions were not framed to assess the occurrence of medically determined gynecological problems. Instead, they elicited women's perceptions of bio medically-defined morbidities that they were experiencing.

1.9 Data Types

Socio-demographic data have been collected from 559 ever-married women, of reproductive age groups (between 15-49 years) and their children (0-4 years). The demographic parameters suggested by WHO scientific Group (1964) have been taken into consideration. These are as follows:

Individual information: These include name, age, sex, marital status, place of residence religious beliefs etc. of the informants from 559 households.

Fertility and reproductive health behaviour: Includes pregnancy history of every ever-married women, age at marriage, present age of mother, age at first and last child birth, age at menarche and menopause, total number of live births, birth order, age and sex of child, place of delivery, ante-natal care. Data on reproductive performance have been collected from 559 ever-married women between (15-49) years.

Child health and morbidity pattern: Includes data on number of children living, common aliment symptoms and diagnosed diseases, treatment availability and practices, breastfeeding practices and duration by age, gender and other characteristics. Data have been recorded on 221 children (0-4) years of age.

Socio-economic traits: These include occupational and educational status of the informants.

Self-reported symptoms of gynecological problems:

The disorders associated with the self-reported symptoms are as follows:

1. Anemia: Feeling excessively weak, tired, or breathless during normal household activities.

2. Menstrual disorders: Heavy or light irregular bleeding; painful menstruation, or spotting between periods.

3. Acute pelvic inflammatory disease (PID): Lower abdominal pain or vaginal discharge with fever.

4. Hemorrhoids: Pain or bleeding while passing stools.

5. Dyspareunia: Pain during intercourse.

6. Lower reproductive tract infection: White or colored discharge from the vagina with bad odor, itching, or irritation.

7. Urinary tract infection: Abnormal frequency of urination, with burning sensation while passing urine.

8. Prolapse: Feeling of something (a mass or swelling) coming from the vagina, or leakage of urine when coughing or sneezing.

9. Fistula: Constant leaking of feces or urine from the vagina.

No claims have been made in this study about the diagnostic accuracy of these symptoms. The relationships between self-reported symptoms and clinically verifiable conditions in this study are uncertain. Some of the symptoms reported here might not be gynecological in nature. However, the symptom categories are suggestive of the corresponding medical conditions and, in terms of clinical practice, warrant referral for detailed examination and laboratory testing. The questions about pain during intercourse were dropped because information on this topic proved difficult to collect. The questions about other symptoms were included in the main questionnaire. Regardless of the imprecise correspondence between these women's reported symptoms and medically verifiable conditions, their perceived ill health is important in its own because it determines their health-seeking behavior. An attempt has been made to produce micro level findings. There are certain gaps and therefore the conclusion derived cannot be comprehensive in nature.

1.10 Ethical considerations:

All the individuals selected in the sample for the present study provided their

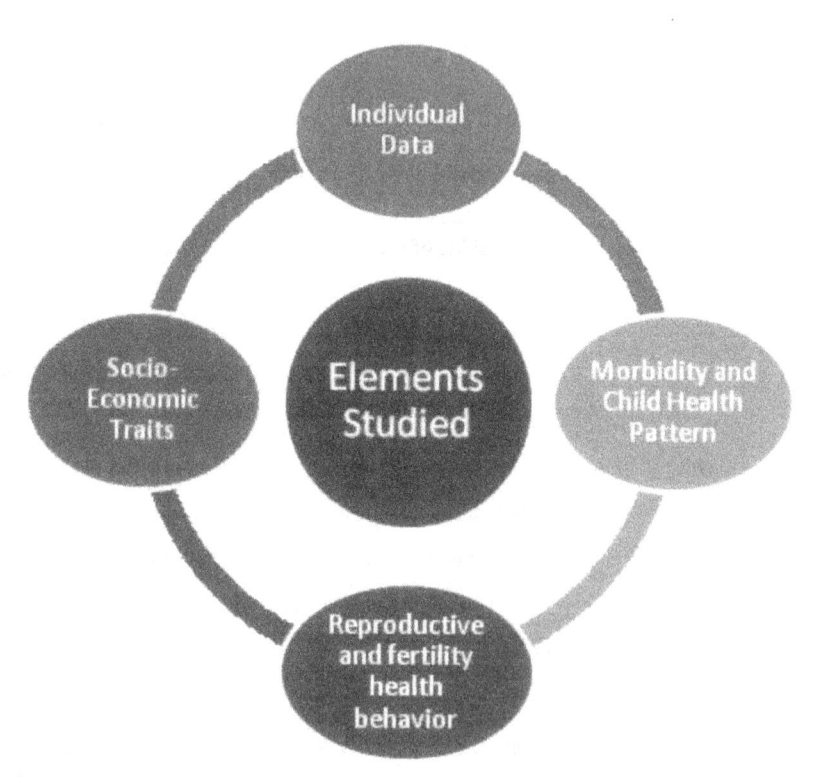

Figure 3: Schematic Framework for the study

consent voluntarily. This work was approved by the Indian Council of Medical Research ethical review board.

1.11 Overview of the thesis

This study is focused on the health conditions of the women and children living in abject poverty in the slums of Kolkata. In Chapter one, the slums of Kolkata has been discussed in relation with urbanization. The aim and scope of the study has also been introduced along with a comprehensive review of the literatures on this topic. The chapter also deals with the research methodologies and the approaches for collecting data. The second chapter discusses about various aspects of slums in Kolkata including area, population. It includes a brief history of Kolkata city and the slums. It also gives the details about socio-economic and household characteristics including quality of life, poverty level and vulnerability in slums of Kolkata. Chapter three portrays the socio-economic life of the slum women in Kolkata, along with the socio-demographic indicators which mainly focus on the health condition of the women living in slum areas. Chapter four provides detailed account of the issues of fertility and reproductive health behaviour of the slum women. Along with this it also explains about the barriers in accessing the system of health delivery and the challenges in adopting the health delivery systems. Chapter five gives a holistic view of the health conditions, diseases and treatment availed by the slum women. The chapter six discusses about the child health and diseases common among the slum children; breastfeeding practices and immunization coverage within slums. The seventh chapter deals with the hypothesis testing by the analysis of data. In chapter eight, the summary and conclusions based on the study and future directions for research are presented.

Chapter 2

Kolkata city and Slums

As per Census of India, population of Kolkata in 2011 is 4,580,544 of which male and female are 2,506,029 and 2,074,515 respectively.

Table 2.1: Demographic Profile of Kolkata

Description			
City	Kolkata		
Government	Municipal Corporation		
Urban Agglomeration	Kolkata Metropolitan		
Kolkata City	**Total**	**Male**	**Female**
City Population(adults)	**4,580,544**	2,506,029	2,074,515
Children (0-6)	**339,323**	175,564	163,759
Literates	**3,588,137**	1,926,915	1,661,222
Average Literacy (%)	**86.31 %**	88.34 %	84.06 %
Sex ratio	**908**		
Child Sex ratio	**933**		

Source: The office of The Registrar General & Census Commissioner, India.

2.1 Kolkata – a brief history

During the early days of British rule in India, Kolkata (previously Calcutta) was the capital of the country, but later the British rulers shifted the capital to Delhi, the present capital of India. Kolkata is now the capital of the state of West Bengal. It is well circulated that Job Charnok, a British tradesman is the founder of this city, and in August 24, 1690, he found this place as a good landing place and setup an outpost of the East India Company. However recently in an attempt to rewrite the history of the city under the verdict of Honourable Calcutta High Court, the leading historians are of the opinion that no such colonial settlers can be treated as the founder for establishing an old ,prosperous settlement of Kolkata. The then villages of Sutanuti, Gobindapur and Kalikata provided the highland needed for massive business houses, residential quarters, villas and other establishments needed for the administrative commercial activities. However, at the same time it is true that the political and economic importance of Kolkata was grown manifold with the association of the East India Company and the British Raj .The three villages Sutanuti, Gobindapur and Kolkata were parts of an estate belonging to the Mughal Empire, whose Zamindari rights were held by the Sabarna Roy Chowdhury family of Barisha- Behala. Gradually the East India Company increased their territory of occupancy and ultimately in 1765, Shah Alam – I , the then Mughal Emperor granted the right to the East India Company to collect land revenue and administer justice to the Bengal province, including the present day Bihar and Orissa (Nair, 1990).

"Since the days of its inception, the city of Calcutta continues to expand its limit slowly but steadily. At the dawn of the 18th century, 41 villages along with Sutanuti, Kalikata and Gobindapur gave the first shape of Calcutta Municipal area" (Mitra, 1990). "The town continued to grow steadily throughout 18th and 19th centuries and the first 50 years of the present century marked an unprecedented rate of expansion. In 1701 the extension of the city was 1682 acres and in 1953 it went upto 23629 acres" (Mitra,

1990). At present the city proper, that is, the area under the Kolkata Municipal Corporation is now 187.33 square kilometres with a population of 3.3 million in 1981 which steadily rose to 4.5 million in 2011.Throughout the 19th century the city area expanded in conformity with its rapidly increasing population, but first half of the 20th century, it witnessed an unprecedented growth in both size and population. According to 1901 census, 68.15% of the total city population comprised immigrants, of them 52.2 % came from interior district of Bengal, 14.8 % from other parts of India, and remaining 1.1% from outside the country. " Centuries ago, colonial and trading interests gave birth to the city of Calcutta and this made it the focal point of intensive economic activities . The city together with its vast hinterland attracted multiple industries which enhanced the scope of employment" (Mitra, 1990). Kolkata had long been the second capital of the British Empire and its primacy in the Eastern hemisphere obviously had a great impact on the socio economic growth. Gradually the city of Calcutta became a centre of job and this pulled job-seekers from nearby districts and states. In 1911, there were 6,24,000 workers accounting for three fifth of the total city population. The extent of predominance of immigrant earners in Kolkata's occupational structure remains unchanged throughout the first six decades of the 20th century. In 1961, the percentage of workers among residents and migrant groups were 29.7% and 70.2% respectively (Mitra, 1990). A majority of the immigrants came from the districts of Bengal, mostly from 24 Parganas, Howrah, Midnapore, etc. The Bengali immigrants of Kolkata accounted for 3, 41,000 persons in 1911 and their number steadily increased to 11, 63,716 in 1951. As the bulk of Bengali migrants came from neighbouring districts, they moved into the city with their families, considerably enhancing the number of dependents among these populations.

2.2 Religion

Hinduism is the major religion in Kolkata city with 76.51 % followers. Islam is second most popular religion with approximately 20.60 % followers. In the city, Christianity is followed by 0.88 %, Jainism by 0.47 %, Sikhism by 0.31 % and Buddhism by 0.31 %.

Table: 2.2: Population of Kolkata by different religious beliefs

Description	Total	Percentage
Hindu	3,440,290	76.51 %
Muslims	926,414	20.60 %
Not Stated	48,982	1.09 %
Christian	39,758	0.88 %
Jain	21,178	0.47 %
Sikh	13,849	0.31 %
Buddhist	4,771	0.11 %
Others	1,452	0.03 %

2.3 Kolkata Slums:

The total slums in Kolkata city numbers 300,755 in which population of 1,490,811 resides. This is around 32.55% of total population of Kolkata. This implies that almost one-third of Kolkata's population are living in slums as tabulated below.

Table 2.3 : Total Population and Slum Population of Kolkata by sex.

	TOTAL POPULATION	MALE	FEMALE	SLUM POPULATION	MALE	FEMALE
Kolkata CITY	4,580,544	2,506,029	2,074,515	1,490,811	825,334	665,477

Source: The office of The Registrar General & Census Commissioner, India.

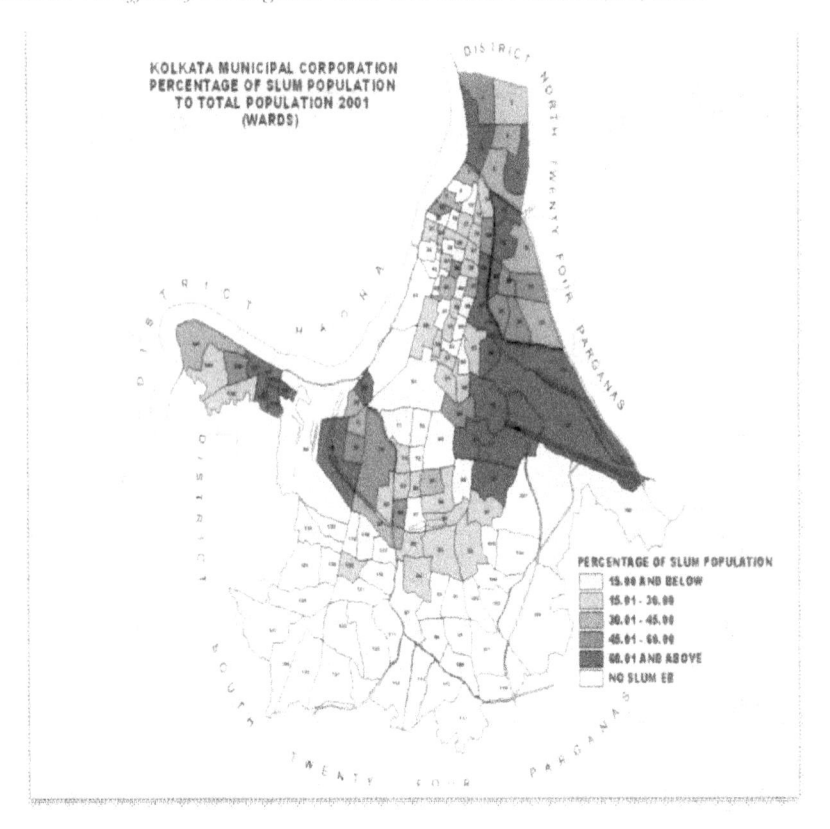

Figure 3: Map Showing Percentage of Slum Population to Total Population in different wards of Kolkata Municipal Corporation. (Source: Office of the Registrar General & Census Commissioner, India, 2001.)

2.4 Slums - meaning and types

First appearing during the 1820s in London, the term 'slum' was used to identify the poorest quality housing areas and living in the most unsanitary conditions. Terms such as slum, shanty, squatter settlement and low-income community are now used interchangeably. The term used in India for slums are chawls (Mumbai, Ahmadabad), katras/jhuggi/jhopdi (Delhi), zopadpattis (Maharashtra, Gujarat) and bustee (Kolkata). Outside India various terms like favela (Brazil), rookery (London), gecekondu (Turkey), villa (Argentina), skid row, barrio, ghetto are used to mean slum.

For the first time in Census 2001, slum areas were earmarked across the country, particularly, in cities and towns having population of 50,000 or above. West Bengal is among the top populous states in India with a population of 64, 18,594, residing in 13, 91,756 (absolute number) households in slums.

Though the Registrar General of India has defined slum as, "A street, alley, etc that is located in the crowded district of the city and is mainly inhabited by the poor class", the Central Statistics Organization (C.S.O) defines slums as an area "having 25 or more katcha structures, mostly of temporary nature, or 50 or more households residing mostly in katcha structures huddled together or inhabited by persons with practically no private latrine and inadequate public latrine and water facilities".

L.W. Riley et.al (2007) described slum as "A congested urban residential area that is mainly characterized through the deteriorated unsanitary buildings, social disorganization and poverty." More recently, Paul and Vasudevan (2010) have described slums "as a compact settlement of around 20 households that are poorly build, mainly of temporary nature, facing unhygienic conditions of drinking water and other facilities, and are most crowded with inadequate sanitation".

Figure 5: A view of Kolkata slum

Three *types* of slums have been defined in Census, namely, Notified, Recognized and Identified.

(i) All notified areas in a town or city notified as 'Slum' by State, Union territories Administration or Local Government under any Act including a 'Slum Act' may be considered as Notified slums

(ii) All areas recognised as 'Slum' by State, Union territories Administration or Local Government, Housing and Slum Boards, which may have not been formally notified as slum under any act may be considered as Recognized slums

(iii) A compact area of at least 300 population or about 60-70 households of poorly built congested tenements, in unhygienic environment usually with inadequate infrastructure and lacking in proper sanitary and drinking water facilities. Such areas should be identified personally by the Charge Officer and also inspected by an officer nominated by Directorate of Census Operations. Such areas may be considered as Identified slums.

2.5 Physical structure of housing in slums

The housing structures in slums are classified into three categories, viz., 'pucca', 'semi-pucca' and 'katcha' in the NSSO surveys. The 49th Round of National Sample Survey Organisation (NSSO) survey highlights that at all-India level, the dwelling units were distributed equally, i.e 1/3rd (approximately) under each category, viz. pucca, semi pucca and katcha housing structure. Here 'Pucca' means those with both roof and walls made of pucca materials such as cement, Concrete, oven-burnt bricks and other such building reinforcement materials. 'Katcha' means those with both roof and walls made of katcha (non-pucca) materials, such as mud, thatch, bamboo, tents, etc. 'Semi-pucca' means those with either roof or walls, but not both, made of pucca materials.

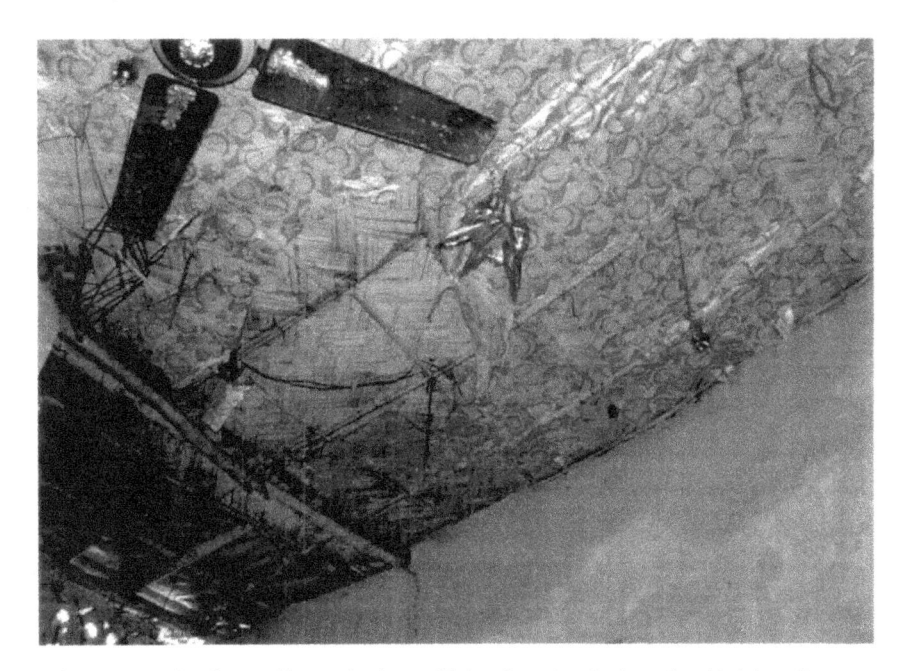

Figure 6 A ' Semi pucca' house in slum with bamboo-thatched roof and brick wall

Figure 7 A club in the slum-area

Figure 8 The entrance to the studied slum-area

2.6 Attributes of Slums

A review of the various approaches used by national and local governments and institutions involved in slum issues reveals the following attributes of slums:

1. Lack of basic services – lack of access to improved sanitation facilities and improved water source, supplemented sometimes, by the absence of waste collection systems, electricity supply, surfaced roads and footpaths, street lighting and drainage.

2. Sub-standard Dwelling- High number of substandard housing structures often built with non-permanent materials unsuitable for housing, given local conditions of location and climate, e.g. earthen floors, mud-and-wattle walls, thatched roofs, etc. – often in violation of housing norms and standards locally applicable.

Figure 9 'Semi-pucca' dwelling hut in slum

3. Over-crowding and High Density- Very low space per person, high occupancy rate, co-habitation by different families and a large number of single-room units. Often five and more persons share a one-room unit for cooking, sleeping and living.

4. Unhealthy/Hazardous Conditions- Unhealthy living conditions due to lack of basic services - open sewers, lack of pathways, uncontrolled dumping of waste, polluted environment, etc. Houses may be built on hazardous lands, unsuitable for settlement, such as floodplains, drains, river beds, garbage dumps, and on areas prone to landslide.

5. Insecure Tenure/Informal Settlements-Lack of formal document entitling the occupant to inhabit the land or structure - illegality of living; informal or unplanned settlements cropping up on public lands or lands reserved for non-residential purposes.

6. Poverty and Exclusion- Income poverty is sometimes considered a characteristic of slum-dwellers, but not always. Slum conditions are physical and due to statutory and regulatory factors that create barriers to human and social development.

7. Minimum Settlement Size- The municipal slum definition of Kolkata requires a minimum of 700 square metres to be occupied by huts. Census of India 2001 requires at least 300 people or 60-70 households living in a settlement cluster.

2.7 Socio-economic and Household Characteristics of the Kolkata slums:

In more than 72 percent of slums in Kolkata, the majority of the houses were built by pucca materials. In the present study, data on housing, amenities and household characteristics were gathered from 559 households in four different slums.

2.7.1 Solid Waste Disposal:

Data collected for analyzing social and environmental background reflect poor living conditions of these households of the slum area. Leaving minimal population, majority of them stay in an unhygienic surrounding, with lack of appropriate garbage disposal or no waste disposal system. 96.1 % of the respondents agreed that frequency of garbage disposal is not satisfactory as it appears from the table and figure below.

Figure 10 Garbage removal in slum

Table 2.4 Frequency and Percentage distribution of garbage removal and waste disposal in surrounding areas of the slum households

		\multicolumn{4}{c	}{Solid waste disposal in slums}
		Frequency	Percent	Valid Percent	Cumulative Percent
Valid	Present	22	3.9	3.9	3.9
	Absent	537	96.1	96.1	100.0
	Total	559	100.0	100.0	

Table2.5 Table showing presence /absence of drainage facilities in the slum areas

		\multicolumn{4}{c	}{Drainage System}
		Frequency	Percent	Valid Percent	Cumulative Percent
Valid	Present	30	5.4	5.4	5.4
	Not present	529	94.6	94.6	100.0
	Total	559	100.0	100.0	

2.7.2 Drainage :

Lack of proper drainage system results in rampant water logging in monsoons in these areas. Table 3.5 shows there is almost no sewer drainage facility in the slums. Lack of solid waste management and inadequate sewer drainage are the biggest factors for environmental pollution and health risks in slums.

2.7.3 Number of rooms :

The houses in the studied slums are either *katcha, semi-pucca or pucca* with one (61.5%), two (24.2%), three (5.4%) and more than three (2.1%) rooms , as table no:3.6 illustrates. The Katcha houses comprise of mud walls and roofs made of tiles and asbestos and are devoid of any exclusive room (7%).

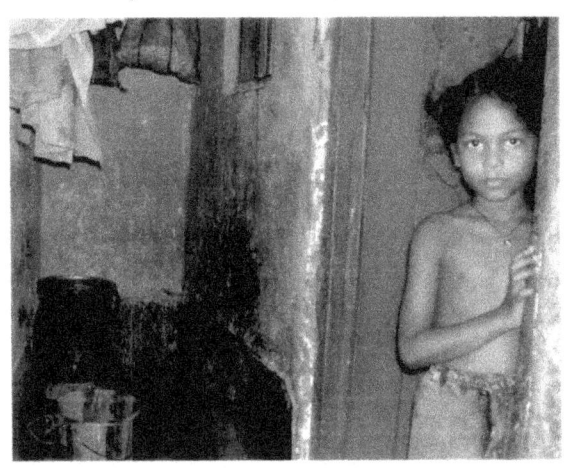

Figure 11 A child in slum house

Figure 12 Slum lane

Table 2.6 : Frequency and percentage distribution of number of rooms

		Frequency	Percent	Valid Percent	Cumulative Percent
Valid	No exclusive room	38	6.8	6.8	6.8
	One room	344	61.5	61.5	68.3
	Two rooms	135	24.2	24.2	92.5
	Three rooms	30	5.4	5.4	97.9
	More than 3	12	2.1	2.1	100.0
	Total	559	100.0	100.0	

Number of rooms in slum households

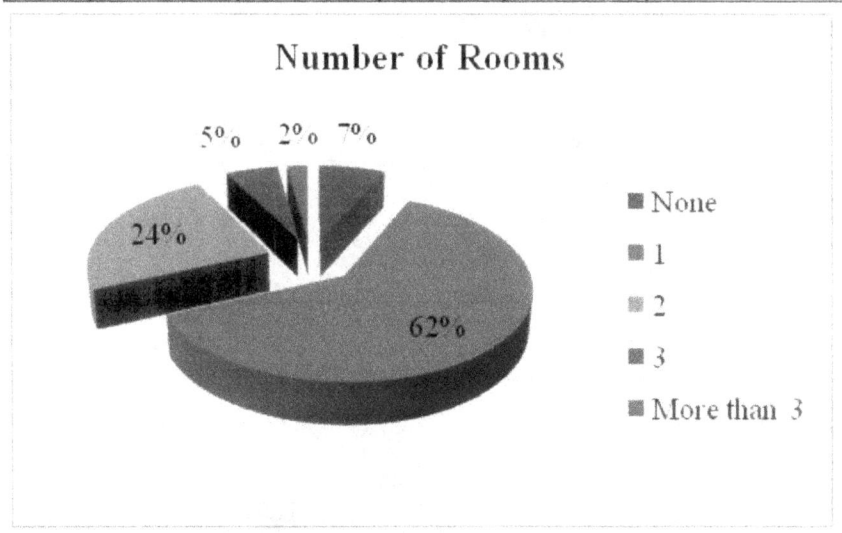

Figure 13 : Graphical representation of number of rooms of each slum household.

2.7.4 Ventilation :

The slum households also lack appropriate ventilation systems. Though 93% of the respondents said that their shelters contains windows/ventilators and only 7% of them denied to such facility, yet, most of the settlements were devoid of proper ventilators or windows which enables effective air circulation. 7% of the respondents who denied having any ventilation, mostly stayed in jhupris made of plastic and not of brick or mud and thus, they were more of temporary structures.

Figure 14 Slum house ventilation

Table 2.7: Frequency and percentage distribution of presence of windows and ventilators

		Frequency	Percent	Valid Percent	Cumulative Percent
Valid	Present	520	93.0	93.0	93.0
	Absent	39	7.0	7.0	100.0
	Total	559	100.0	100.0	

Windows and Ventilators

Out of 93% respondents who said to have ventilation in their houses, 79.1 % had only one window, 11.6% had two windows and only 2.3% had more than 2 windows as shown in the table 3.8 and followed by the graph.

Table 2.8: Frequency and percentage distribution of number of windows and ventilators present in slum households

Number and Frequency of windows/ventilators present in households

		Frequency	Percent	Valid Percent	Cumulative Percent
Valid	1	442	79.1	85.0	85.0
	2	65	11.6	12.5	97.5
	More than 2	13	2.3	2.5	100.0
	Total	520	93.0	100.0	
Absent		39	7.0		
Total		559	100.0		

Quantity of windows /ventilators in each households

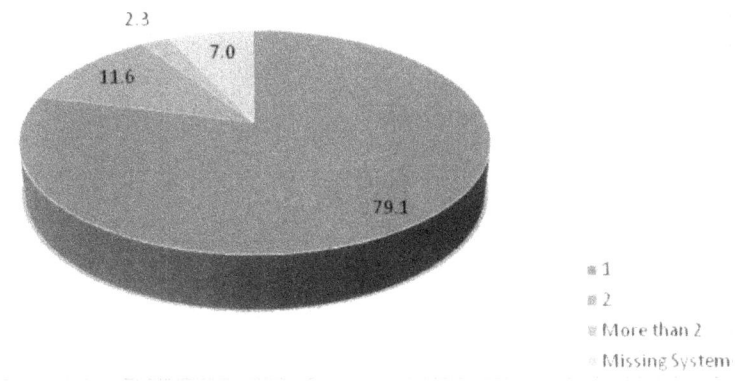

- 1
- 2
- More than 2
- Missing System

Values: 2.3, 7.0, 11.6, 79.1

Figure 15 : Graphical representation of the presence of windows/ventilators in slums.

2.7.5 Lighting :

A glance at the source of lighting suggests that most of the slum households have electricity connections (85%), while some of them are still using kerosene (10%), or other forms of oils (1.7%). Very few of them have solar lights (1.2%) while a small percentage (1.4%) do not have proper means of lighting.

Table 2.9: Frequency and percentage distribution of source of lighting

	Source of Lighting				
		Frequency	Percent	Valid Percent	Cumulative Percent
Valid	Electricity	475	84.9	84.9	84.9
	Kerosene	60	10.8	10.8	95.7
	Solar energy	7	1.2	1.2	96.9
	Other forms of lighting	9	1.7	1.7	98.6
	No lighting system	8	1.4	1.4	100.0
	Total	559	100.0	100.0	

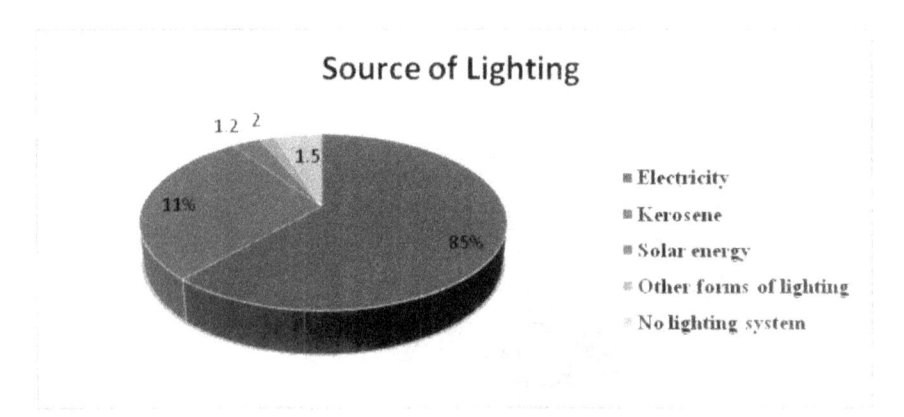

Figure 16: Graphical representation of the source of lighting in the slum households

Figure 17 A slum household with electricity

2.7.6 Drinking water:

Next we take a look into the different sources of drinking water in the slums. Most of the households use tap water (82%) for consumption, while some use hand pumps (13%) to collect drinking water. Among the other sources of drinking water are tube wells /bore wells located nearby their houses mostly outside their premises. Drinking water is sometimes also collected from pipes or supplied by tankers (1.3%).

Table 2.10: Frequency and percentage distribution of source of drinking water

		Source of drinking water in slums			
		Frequency	Percent	Valid Percent	Cumulative Percent
Valid	Tap	460	82.3	82.3	82.3
	Hand Pump	72	12.9	12.9	95.2
	Other sources	7	1.3	1.3	96.4
	Tubewell/ borehole	20	3.6	3.6	100.0
	Total	559	100.0	100.0	

Figure 18 Source of potable water in slum

Figure 19 A child drinking water from its source

2.7.7 Sanitation :

After housing and water, sanitation holds the key importance for healthy living. From the table 2.11 and table 2.12 we can have an idea of the bathing and latrine facilities available in the slums.

Table: 2.11 Availability of Bathing Facility within slum premises

Bathing Facility	Frequency	Percentage of Households
1. Have facility	442	79.0
(a) Bathroom	372	66.5
(b) Enclosure without roof	70	12.5
2. Does not have facility	117	21.0
Total	559	100.0

Table 2.11 shows that though majority of the households have some kind of bathing facility (almost 80%), the enclosure is sometimes without a roof. A large section of households (21%) are even without a bathing facility where the dwellers are forced to bath and wash in the open. Thus menstrual hygiene is a problem for many adolescent girls and women, who lack the privacy to properly wash and dry menstrual rags. Using wet rags result in infection.

Figure 20 Open bathing space in slum house

Figure 21 A girl washing clothes in slum house

Availability of Bathing Facility within slum premises

■ Frequency ■ Percentage of Households

Category	Frequency	Percentage of Households
Total	559	100
2. Does not have facility	117	21
(b) Enclosure without roof	70	12.5
(a) Bathroom	372	66.5
1. Have facility	442	79

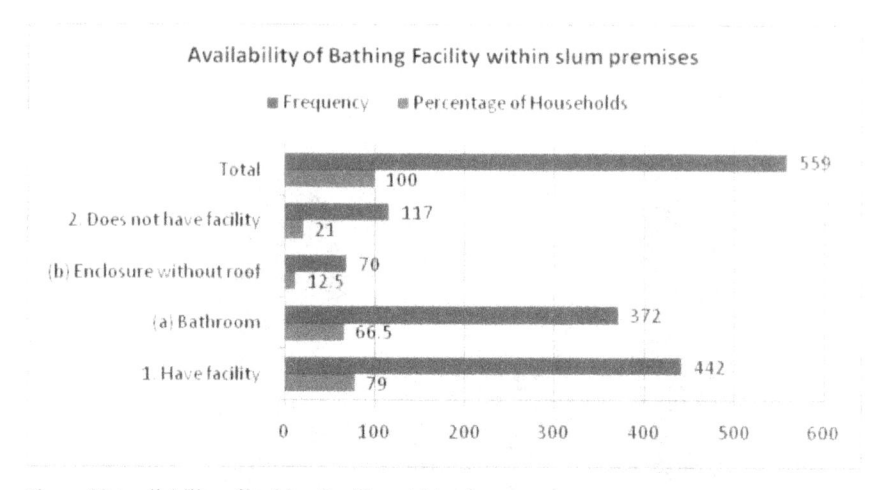

Figure 22 Availability of bathing Facility within slum premises

Figure 23 Toilet facility inside a house in slum

Figure 24 An open urinal in slum

Table 2.12 Availability of Latrine Facility in slum households

Types of Latrines	Frequency	Percentage of Households
1. Latrine within the premises	330	59.0
(a) Water closet	297	53.0
(b) Pit latrine	33	6.0
2. No latrine within premises	229	41.0
(a) Public latrine	168	30.0
(b) Open	61	11.0
Total	559	100.0

Table 2.12 shows the availability of Latrine Facility in slum households. It is unfortunate to note that though almost 60 percent of the slum households have latrine facilities with their premises, a very high percentage (41%) still lack the latrine facilities. Most of the slum dwellers (30%) are either forced to use the public latrine or have to go to the open areas (11%). Hygiene awareness and knowledge of the links between poor hygiene and disease are lowest among the slum dwellers. Poor sanitation contributes to high levels of water-borne diseases like jaundice and diarrhoea among the children living in the slums.

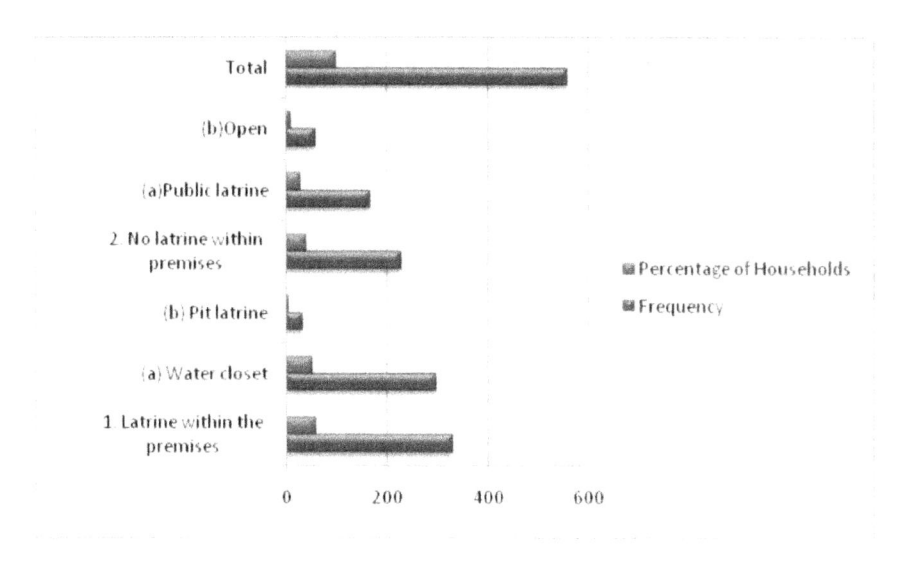

Figure 25 The availability of Latrine Facility in slums of Kolkata

2.8 Household expenditure pattern in Kolkata slums:

From the Kolkata Study Report April 2014, it has been revealed that the Expenditure pattern of Kolkata slums is comparatively high on medical and food items than the West Bengal urban population. The report on Government led exclusion of the urban poor, 2014 reveals that Kolkata slums spend 54.81% of their expenditure on food and intoxicants against 8.71% by West Bengal urban. Kolkata slums spend 2.40% on housing whereas West Bengal urban spends 20.34% on housing. Kolkata slums spend 6.26% on education whereas West Bengal urban spends 5.49% on education. Kolkata slums spend 11.81% on healthcare facilities which is very high whereas West Bengal urban spends 5.32%.

Data collected from the present field study are in tandem with the findings of this report. It has been found that the slum dwellers spend a major part (54.9 %) of their expenditure on food and intoxicants, which is considered to be very high, whereas they spend very less (only 5.51%) of their expenditure on housing. Expenses on health care are also relatively high (17.5%), while reasons like marriage or repayment of loans are causes of other major expenses among the slum dwellers of Kolkata.

Table 2.13 Expenditure pattern of Kolkata slum households.

Expenditure of slum Households	Percentage of expenses	Cumulative Percentage
Housing	5.51	5.51
Food	54.93	60.44
Education	9.10	69.54
Health	17.45	86.99
Other reasons	13.01	100.0

Percentage of Household expenses

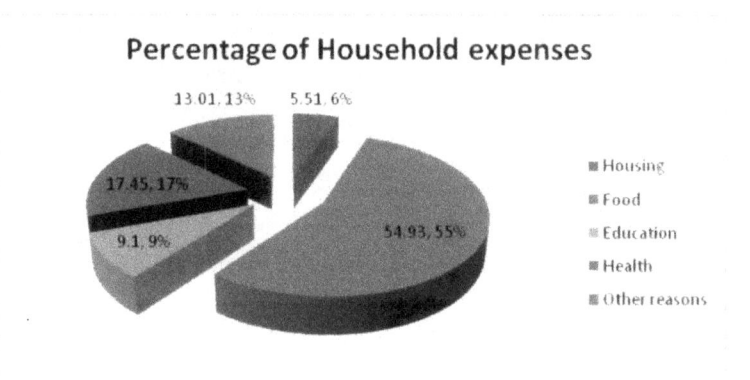

Figure 26 Graphical Representation of the Expenditure pattern in Kolkata slums

Figure 27 A slum family

These findings show that State support may be needed for slum dwellers in health and education at all levels. Staying in slum areas, their expenditure is very high towards the food items and healthcare and low on rental. Hence, relocating to far places for rehabilitation and resettlement of slum dwellers may make their earning unsustainable. This is a complex issue having many dimensions. When the state recognizes this, it should ensure that access to basic amenities of drinking water, sanitation, hygiene, public health and education is not compromised. Present level of investment in these needs to be augmented and expedited.

Chapter 3

The Slum Women and Children

Around 1.5 million people in Kolkata live in the slums which constitute almost one-third of the total city population (as per Census2011, India). In terms of survival and well-being, the slum women and children are the most vulnerable. Exposure to factors such as deteriorating urban environment, poor housing, lack of sanitation, low income, lack of safe drinking water and poor nutritional status influence the burden of disease and their health outcomes. The women often have to struggle for basic resources to feed their families, doing informal sector work and employing themselves as domestic-helps. Most of women try to balance their life between family care-taking and economic activities, but in this work and family life balance they have to compromise on health, which is further worsened by deteriorating, overcrowded and unhygienic environment of these areas. Their children are far worse-off, suffering from malnutrition, diarrhea, infections, and jaundice coupled with educational deprivation. In this chapter an overview of the studied population in terms of their basic demographic characteristics and socio-economic conditions affecting their general health has been attempted.

3.1 Demographic profile of the sample population

The important characteristics of the studied slum population including age-sex structure, marital status, educational status, occupational pursuits, income, working hours, which are helpful in understanding the basic living conditions of the slum population have been discussed here.

3.1 Age –Sex Structure of the total population: The age and sex structure of the total slum population with the corresponding sex-ratios is given in the table below:

Table 3.1 Age-sex structure of the total population with age-specific sex ratios.

AGE COHORT (IN YEARS)	MALE POPULATION NO.	%	FEMALE POPULATION NO.	%	TOTAL POPULATION NO.	%	AGE-SPECIFIC SEX RATIO
0 TO 4	230	13.28	195	11.72	425	12.5	847.8
5 TO 9	269	15.53	201	12.08	470	13.8	747.2
10 TO 14	224	12.93	178	10.70	402	11.8	794.6
15 TO 19	190	10.97	200	12.02	390	11.5	1052.6
20 TO 24	230	13.28	229	13.76	459	13.5	995.6
25 TO 29	173	9.99	185	11.12	358	10.5	1069.3
30 TO 34	123	7.10	130	7.81	253	7.4	1056.9
35 TO 39	90	5.20	94	5.65	184	5.4	1044.4
40 TO 44	73	4.21	85	5.11	158	4.7	1164.3
45 TO 49	77	4.45	106	6.37	183	5.4	1376.6
50 TO 54	41	2.37	44	2.64	85	2.5	1073.1
55 TO 59	5	0.29	8	0.48	13	0.4	1600.0
60 TO 64	3	0.17	4	0.24	7	0.2	1333.3
65 Above	4	0.23	5	0.30	9	0.3	1250.0
TOTAL	1732	100.00	1664	100.00	3396	100.0	960.7

Table 3.1 represents the detailed age and sex structure of the total population living in the four slums of Kolkata. 38.1% of the total population are below 15 years of age with a sex composition revealing a deficit of female child. The concentration of the population between 15 to 34 years age groups is very high (43%) and only about 9 % of the population belong to above 45 years age groups. The sex ratio reveals that in the age-groups between 0-14 years there is preponderance of male children whereas in the age groups above 15 years, there is preponderance of females. Therefore it is observed that among the slum dwellers in Kolkata there are female preponderances over the males in the adult age groups. It is also noticed that population above 65 years is very negligible. It points out to the prevalence of high birth rate and high death rate among the slum populations.

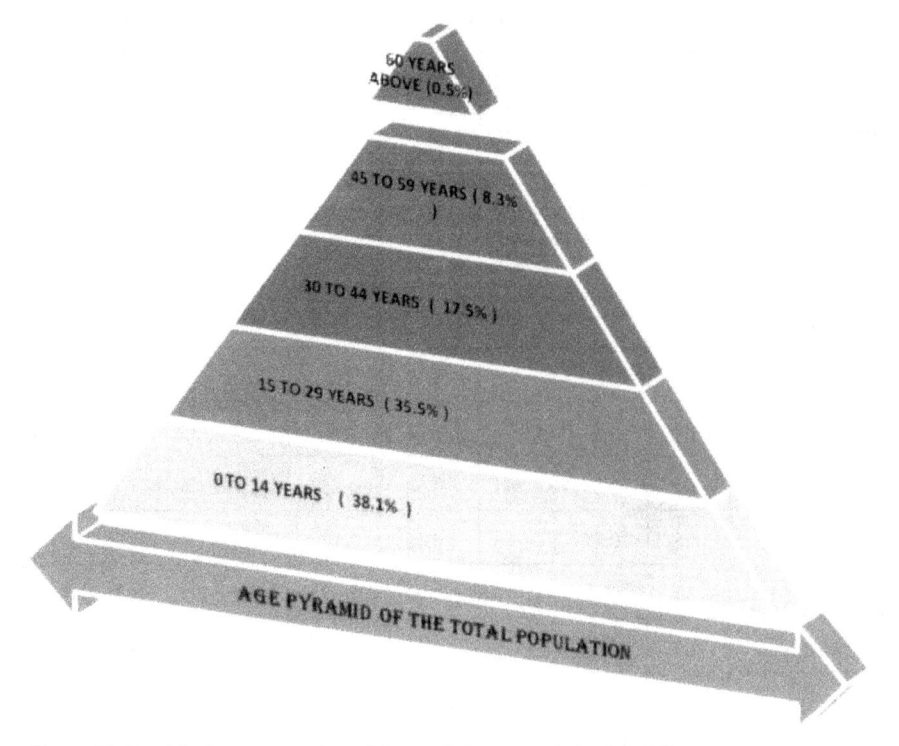

Figure 28 Graphical representation of the total slum population by different age groups.

3.2 Age structure of the female population:

This study is focused on women (between 15-49 years) and their children (0-4 years). Table 3.2 shows the age structure of the studied female population (559 in number) in the slums, belonging between 15 to 49 years of age groups. Out of all the groups, women within the age range of 20 to 34 years are present in majority (over 66%). A small portion of the women belong to the 15-19 age group (5%) and 40-49 age group (15%).

Table 3.2 Age structure of the studied female population

AGE GROUPS	TOTAL NUMBER (N)	PERCENT FREQUENCY DISTRIBUTION
15 TO 19	27	4.83%
20 TO 24	113	20.21%
25 TO 29	132	23.61%
30 TO 34	122	21.82%
35 TO 39	80	14.31%
40 TO 44	41	7.33%
45 TO 49	44	7.87%
TOTAL	559	100.00%

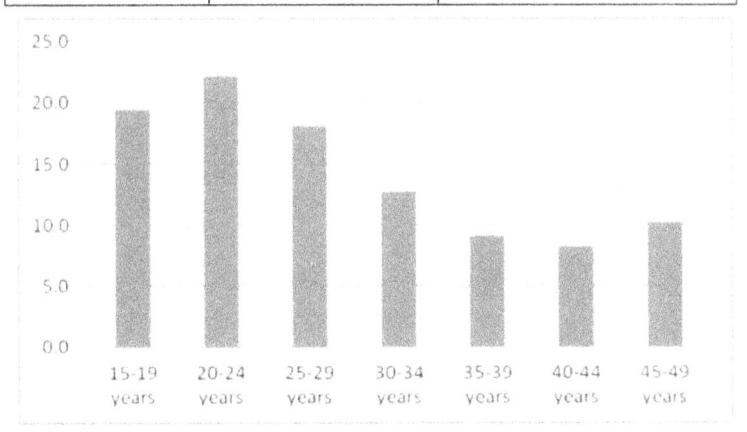

Figure 29 Distribution of the studied female population by different age groups.

3.3. Age –sex structure of the child population:

The table below depicts the age –sex distribution of the slum-children between 0-4 years of age, born to the ever-married women understudy.

Table 3.3   Age-sex distribution of the child population (0-4 years) in the slums

Age of Child (in months)	Male	Female	Total	Percent Distribution
0-5	12	9	21	9.5
6-11	24	16	40	18.1
12-17	8	4	12	5.5
18-23	28	22	50	22.6
24-29	3	2	5	2.3
30-35	29	20	49	22.1
36-41	2	2	4	1.8
42-47	28	12	40	18.1
Total	134	87	221	100.0

From table 3.3 it is found that there are 221 children (born to 559 ever-married women) belonging to the age groups 0-4 years in the slums of which 60% are males and rest of them are females (40%). 28% of the children are below twelve months, i.e. one year of age, 52 % are between 12-35 months, i.e. 2-3 years and 20% are between 36-47 months, i.e. 3-4 years.

Figure 30 A slum woman with her child

3.4 Marital Status:

As the study is focused on women having one or more offsprings, only the ever-married population is considered. Therefore the unmarried females are not considered as a part of the present study. Table 3.4 represents the marital status of the studied population in different age groups. Among all the ever-married female population (559 in number), 86.2% is currently married, while 14% are presently either separated or widowed.

Table 3.4: Distribution of marital status of females belonging to different age groups

MARITAL STATUS OF FEMALE POPULATION OF REPRODUCTIVE AGEGROUPS

AGE GROUPS	MARRIED	WIDOWED	SEPARATED/ /DIVORCED DESERTED	TOTAL NUMBER	PERCENT REQUENCY DISTRIBUTION
15 TO 19	27	0	0	27	4.83
20 TO 24	112	0	1	113	20.21
25 TO 29	105	0	27	132	23.61
30 TO 34	106	2	14	122	21.82
35 TO 39	73	5	2	80	14.31
40 TO 44	22	19	0	41	7.33
45 TO 49	37	6	1	44	7.87
TOTAL	482	32	45	559	100.00

Table 3.4 shows most of the married population (80%) is between the ages of 20-39 years. It is important to note that a small percentage (5%) of the females between 15-19 years are also married. It points out to the fact that the girls are married at a very tender age and there is a tendency of child marriage among them. It is also seen that nearly 8% of the female population are deserted or separated and 6 % are widowed. It has been observed through case studies that in most cases these separated women become the head of the household consisting of her children. The figure below shows the frequency distribution of the married population.

Frequency

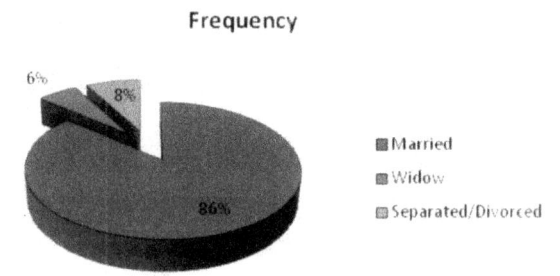

Figure 31 Graphical representation of the marital status of the studied population.

3.5 Educational Standard:

Table 3.5 shows the educational status of the respondents and its distribution on the level of education. Approximately 56% of these women are illiterates. Among the literates, a large portion (35%) is only educated up to the primary level and only a meager percentage could attain higher education (9%).

Table 3.5 Educational status of the studied population

		Frequency	Percent	Valid Percent	Cumulative Percent
Valid	Illiterate	311	55.6	55.6	55.6
	Primary	200	35.8	35.8	91.4
	Secondary	45	8.1	8.1	99.5
	Higher Secondary	1	0.2	0.2	99.6
	Above Higher Secondary	2	0.4	0.4	100.0
	Total	559	100.0	100.0	

Educational Standard

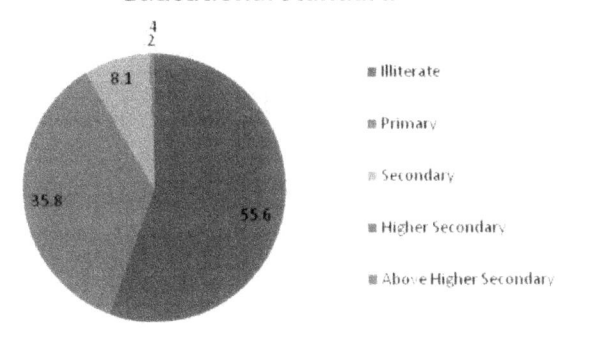

Figure 32 Graphical representation of educational status of the studied population

Figure 33 Slum girls in front of school

Figure 34 "Zari" workers in slum

Table 3.6 Educational status of the female population by age groups and the standard of education

Age of mother In yrs.	Illiterate — Cannot sign	Illiterate — Can sign	Total	Percent	Literate — Primary	Literate — Secondary	Literate — Higher secondary	Literate — Graduation & above	Total	Percent	Grand Total	Percent
15-19	0	5	5	18.52	6	16	0	0	22	81.48	27	100
20-24	0	46	46	40.71	54	12	1	0	67	59.29	113	100
25-29	3	65	68	51.52	54	9	0	1	64	48.48	132	100
30-34	12	72	84	68.85	31	6	0	1	38	31.15	122	100
35-39	15	30	45	56.25	33	2	0	0	35	43.75	80	100
40-44	19	4	23	56.10	18	0	0	0	18	43.90	41	100
45-49	11	29	40	90.91	4	0	0	0	4	9.09	44	100
	60 (10.73)	251 (44.90)	311	55.64	200 (35.78)	45 (8.05)	1 (0.18)	2 (0.36)	248	44.36	559	100

The table 3.6 reveals the educational qualifications of the respondents by age groups and by their educational level. The table reflects a poor condition with majority of them being illiterate (55.6%) with 10.73% of them having no ability to sign their own name, and 44.90% of them possessing the ability to sign their own name in their respective mother tongue. 35.8% (200 in number) possess primary education, 8.1% having secondary level education and near negligible percentage of them— 0.2% and 0.4%, respectively, having qualifications of higher secondary and graduation level. This data reflect a poor condition in educational status of these slum women. The probable causes behind such poor educational standard can be ascertained to their early marriage, lack of motivation and lack of opportunities as the females are often forced to take up odd jobs at an early age for supporting their families financially.

3.6 Occupational pursuits of the studied population: The occupations of the respondents in the slums can be categorized into the following types: Household maids, cooks, ayahs (medical attendants), vegetable or fish vendors, tailors, clerks/peons and others.

Table 3.7 Occupational pursuits of the studied female population

	Occupation				
	Categories	Frequency	Percent	Valid Percent	Cumulative Percent
Valid	Household Work	145	25.9	25.9	25.9
	Clerk/Peon	5	0.9	0.9	26.8
	Maids	298	53.3	53.3	80.1
	Cook	43	7.7	7.7	87.8
	Tailor	10	1.8	1.8	89.6
	Ayah	10	1.8	1.8	91.4
	Petty business/vendors	31	5.5	5.5	97.0
	Other	17	3.0	3.0	100.0
	Total	559	100.0	100.0	

Table 3.7 shows the occupational pursuits of the studied population in slums of Kolkata. Majority of the slum-dwelling women are working as household maids or "kajerloks" (in Bengali) mostly as part-time maid servants, in employer's house. Some of them are exclusively engaged in cooking and others are engaged as ayahs or attendants. These three categories together make a major working force (66%) engaged in domestic services. Some of the slum women are engaged in petty businesses (5%), in shops or do tailoring works (2%). A very small percentage (>1%) are employed in clerical jobs.

Occupation

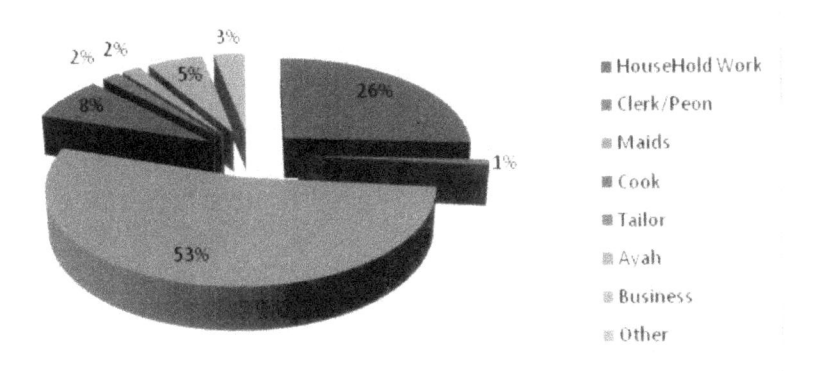

Figure 35 Graphical representation of different types of occupational categories of the women

The above figure shows the various occupational persuits of the slum women. About one-fourth of the respondents are home-makers (25%). These women have no income, although they are engaged in various household works such as washing clothes, cleaning, cooking, and thus they spent more than 15 hours per day in managing such chores but without any monthly monetary benefits.

Figure 36 A women cooking in slum house cum shop.

Table : 3.8 Frequency distribution of the working hours of the respondents

		Total Working Hours			
		Frequency	Percent	Valid Percent	Cumulative Percent
Valid	0-5 hours/day	14	2.5	2.5	2.5
	5-8 hours/day	53	9.5	9.5	12.0
	8-12 hours/day	311	55.6	55.6	67.6
	12-15 hours/day	34	6.1	6.1	73.7
	More than 15 hours/day	147	26.3	26.3	100.0
	Total	559	100.0	100.0	

Women working in household as maids spend on an average 8 to 12 hours in the workplaces and thus have very less time to spend on themselves. Women working in the position of clerks/peons also spend nearly 8 to 12 hours a day in their workplaces, while the women engaged as cooks, tailor and ayah or small business have relatively less working hours. Percentages of women who are working as ayahs in different hospitals, nursing homes and households also have to work minimum for 8 hours a day. The women who stay at home and look after their small children work almost for the entire day (<15 hours) without any wages.

Total Working Hours

- 0-5 hours/day: 9%
- 5-8 hours/day: 56%
- 8-12 hours/day: 6%
- 12-15 hours/day: 26%
- More than 15 hours/day: 3%

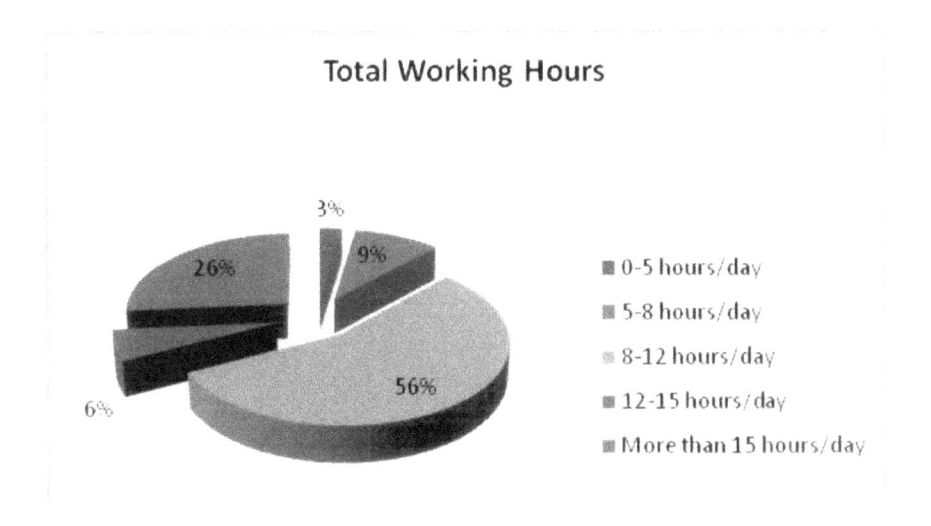

Figure 37 Graphical representation (in percentage) of total working hours by women in slums

3.7 Income:

The average monthly income of the respondents are a little below Rs 3000 per month, however about fifty percent of the respondents may earn about Rs 5000 a month. Table 4.9 gives a detailed distribution of their earning categories of the slum women.

Table 3.9 Income per month generated by the studied women

		Monthly Income			
		Frequency	Percent	Valid Percent	Cumulative Percent
Earnings Valid	>1000 INR/month	152	27.2	27.2	27.2
	1001-2000 INR/month	7	1.3	1.3	28.4
	2001-3000 INR/month	13	2.3	2.3	30.8
	3001-5000 INR/month	84	15.0	15.0	45.8
	More than 5000 INR/month	303	54.2	54.2	100.0
	Total	559	100.0	100.0	

In an average the women normally work for 8 to 12 hours (56%) as household maids and ayahs and earn a monthly income of more than 5000 (54%) Other occupation holders fall mostly in between earning from 1000 to 3000 INR a month. Some maids who work for full-time may earn a monthly income of more than 5000 INR, which is much more than the earning of other occupations, such as cooks, tailors or in small business. But almost one-fourth of them have a meager earning between 1000 to 2000 INR or even lesser.

Monthly Income

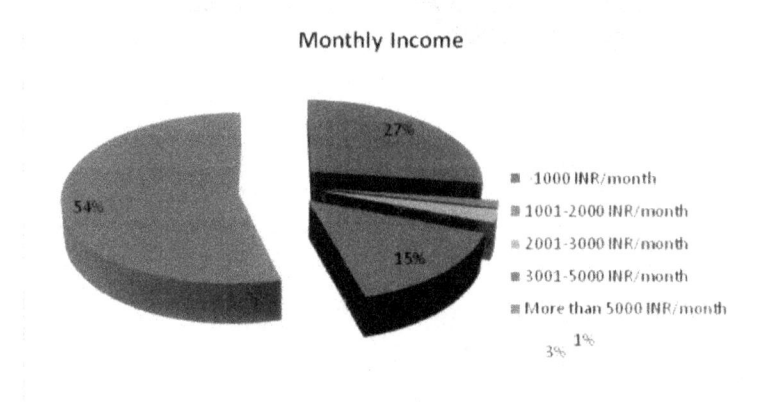

Figure 38 Graphical representation (in percentage) of monthly income earned by the population under study.

Figure 39 Household utensils

Figure 40 Clothes and utensils kept in a slum household

Figure 41 A slum room

Figure 42 A slum woman in bedroom-cum-kitchen

3.8 Travelling Time to work: As the women are employed in different types of work outside the slums, the travelling time is mostly less than half an hour, walking distance. The tables below give the details of the travelling time and distances.

Table 3.10 Time Taken to Travel at work place by the women living in the slums

		Time Taken to Travel			
		Frequency	Percent	Valid Percent	Cumulative Percent
Valid	None	169	30.2	30.2	30.2
	>10 min	81	14.5	14.5	44.7
	10-15 min	99	17.7	17.7	62.4
	15-20 min	158	28.3	28.3	90.7
	20-30 min	52	9.3	9.3	100.0
	Total	559	100.0	100.0	

Table 3.10 shows the time taken by the women dwelling in the slums to travel at their work place. In most of the cases (30%) they work in the nearby areas, and spend little time to reach. But in few cases the distance is more and they spend about 20 minutes in travelling there.

Time taken to travel

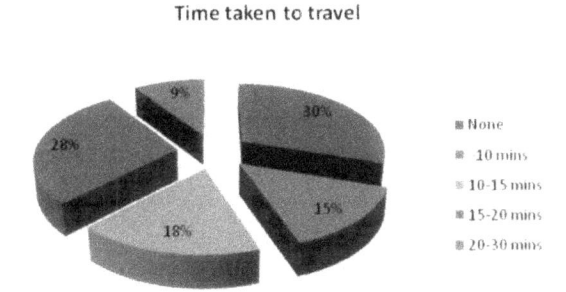

Figure 43 Graphical representation of total time taken (in percentage) to commute by the respondent

3.9 Means of commute:

The slum women who go out to their work place, mostly go by walking, but in some cases they also take the bus or auto or various others means for commuting. These have been discussed below in the table.

Table 3.11 Frequency and percentage distribution of means of commutation

	Means of Commute				
		Frequency	Percent	Valid Percent	Cumulative Percent
Valid	None	229	41.0	41.0	41.0
	Walking	98	17.5	17.5	58.5
	Cycle	107	19.1	19.1	77.6
	Bus	22	3.9	3.9	81.6
	Auto	25	4.5	4.5	86.0
	Local Train	76	13.6	13.6	99.6
	Others	2	0.4	.04	100.0
	Total	559	100.0	100.0	

Table 3.11 shows the various means by which the women commute to their workplace. Nearly 60% of the women are working within walking-distance, and thereby prefer to walk. Some of them work in neighboring localities and take either bus; auto –rickshaws or tram or use cycles (30%). Even some of the women also take local trains to reach their workplace though the percentage is less(14%).The rest of the women who do not commute are either home-makers or work as full-time maids in the houses.

Time taken to travel

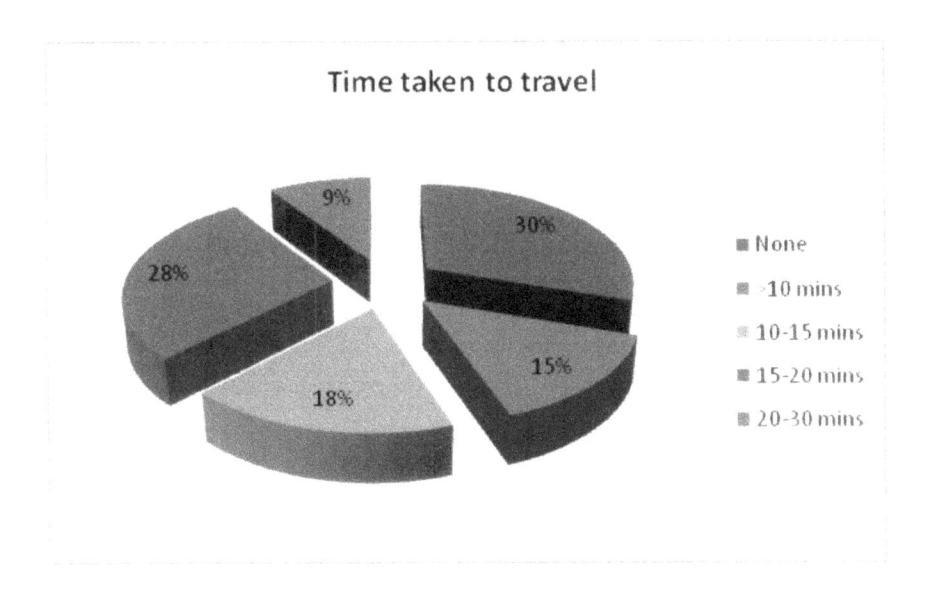

- None: 30%
- >10 mins: 15%
- 10-15 mins: 18%
- 15-20 mins: 28%
- 20-30 mins: 9%

Figure 44 Graphical representation of the various means of commute

Thus in this chapter an attempt has been made to portray the socio-economic life of the slum women.

Chapter 4

Reproductive Health Behaviour

Reproductive health includes the pregnancy history of every ever-married women; their age at marriage, present age of women, age at first and last child birth, age at menarche, total number of live births, birth order, age and sex of child, place of delivery, and ante-natal care. Data on reproductive performance have been collected from 559 ever-married women living in the slums.

An adverse living environment characterised by overcrowding, lack of ventilation in homes, inadequate sanitation and poverty contributes heavily to the occurrences of diseases among the slum women. Socio-demographic attributes including marriage at early age, early pregnancy and low level of literacy also have an impact on the reproductive health of the women. In order to ascertain the reproductive health condition of the women, the following indicators have been studied:

4.1. Age of menarche: Menarche is the primary indicator of onset of sexual maturation in a female that affects her reproductive life. Among the sampled female population, menarche is relatively uncommon before 13 years of age (Table 5.1). Menarcheal age for ever-married women ranges between 11 and 18 years. The median age at menarche is 14.0 years (mean age at menarche is 13.99 years). The mean menarcheal age is almost same as that for lower socio-economic urban Indian population (mean 14.04 years: ICMR, 1982). Thus it can be said that the girls involved in strenuous physical activity of any type as in the urban slums, menarche is delayed (mean 14.16 years).

Table 4.1 : Frequency and percentage distribution of age of menarche among women

Age of menarche			Frequency	Percent	Valid Percent	Cumulative Percent
Valid	10-11 years		5	0.9	0.9	0.9
	12-13 years		189	33.8	33.8	34.7
	14-15 years		274	49.0	49.0	83.7
	16 years and above		91	16.3	16.3	100.0
	Total		559	100.0	100.0	

The table shows that nearly 49% (274) of the total women interviewed had their menarche at their mid-teenage years, i.e., within 14 to 15 years of age. Some of them had within the age range of 12 to 13 years (34%), while few had it after 16 years of age (16%) and very negligible of them (1%) had it during their much younger days, prior to attainment of puberty, within 10-11 years of age.

Age of Menarche

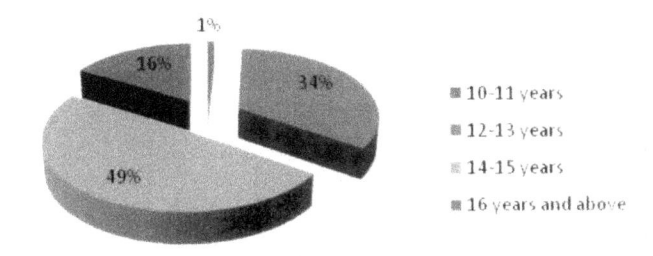

Figure 45 Graphical representation of age of menarche among women

4.2 Age at First marriage: In the present study, age at first marriage refers to age at formal marriage. The median age at first marriage for women aged 15-49 years is 17 years (mean 17.05 years), which is just below the legal permissible age. The study of patterns of age at first marriage indicates that more than three-fourth of the women got married between 15-19 years of age while those marrying before 15 years of age and after 20 years of age is low (Table4.1). It is a reflection of low female educational status. Besides parent's education, family type, age at menarche is some of the factors associated with female age at marriage.

Table: 4.2 Frequency and percentage distribution of age of women at their first marriage

	Age at 1st marriage				
		Frequency	Percent	Valid Percent	Cumulative Percent
Valid	11-14 years	59	10.6	10.6	10.6
	15-17 years	183	32.7	32.7	43.3
	18-21 years	299	53.5	53.5	96.8
	More than 21 years	18	3.2	3.2	100.0
	Total	559	100.0	100.0	

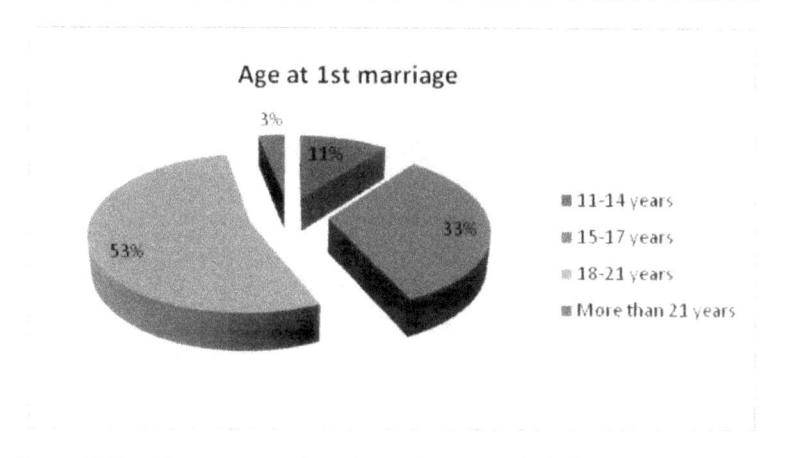

Figure 46 Graphical representation of age of women at their first marriage

Figure 47 Married female respondents at the Chetla slum

4.3. Age of Mothers at First Child Birth:

The onset and cessation of childbearing is important indicator of fertility. Early births are common for ever-married women in the age group 15-19 years (Table 5.3.3). More than 22 percent women aged 15-19 years have given birth to children indicating teenage childbearing. Over half of the women in the age group 45-49 years have had their first childbirth before the age of 20 years, while the corresponding proportion of such women in the age group 20-24 years is two-fifth indicating decline in early child-bearing (before the age of 20 years) during last two and half decades. The median age at first birth is marginally higher for younger women. Overall, the median age at first birth is 19 years (mean 19.59 years) for women aged 15-49 years indicating relatively early marriage and childbearing.

Table 4.3 : Percent distribution of ever married women aged 15-49 years, by age at first childbirth and present age

Mother's age (in years)	No birth	Age at first birth					Total		Median age at birth
		<18	18-19	20-21	22-24	25+	Percent	Number	
15-19	77.8	14.8	7.4	-	-	-	100	27	NC*
20-24	15.9	3.5	36.3	34.5	9.7	-	100	113	19.5
25-29	1.5	9.1	36.4	35.6	16.7	0.8	100	132	19.5
30-34	-	13.1	45.1	27.9	11.5	2.5	100	122	19
35-39	-	17.5	41.3	25	8.8	7.5	100	80	19
40-44	-	2.4	43.9	26.8	22	4.9	100	41	20
45-49	-	30.2	23.3	18.6	25.6	2.3	100	44	19

NC* Not calculated because less than 50 percent of women have had a first child birth

4.4 Age of women at their last child birth

The age at last childbirth (for women aged 40-49 years) is also equally important determinant of fertility. It is suggestive that childbearing is virtually complete by these age-groups. Four-fifth of the women had completed their childbearing by age 30 in the age group 40-44 years with median age at 26 years (Table 4.4). The childbearing was completed by 30 years of age, for more than half women in age group 45-49 years, with 29 years as median age at last childbirth.

Table 4.4 : Percent distribution of ever married women aged 40-49 years, by age at last childbirth and present age

Mother's age at present	Age at last birth (in years)					Total		Median age at last birth
	>25	25-29	30-34	35-39	40+	Percentage	Number	
40-44	22	58.5	14.6	4.9	-	100	41	26
45-49	7	48.8	37.2	7	-	100	44	29

No one reported having a birth after age of 39 years indicating that generally childbearing is complete by this age. Thus it may be inferred that the sampled slum women are reproductively active during prime childbearing ages of 19 to 29 years.

4.5 Number of Children Ever- born and Living: The total number of children ever born to a women and the number of children presently living or surviving is another major health indicator. There were 3.2 induced abortions and 3.5 stillbirths for every 100 live births among the female population of the slums of Kolkata. Majority of pregnancies resulted in live births (85.5 percent) as compared to reproductive loss (14.6 percent).

From the table-4.5 it is found that the ever-married slum women in the childbearing years have borne an average of 3.34 children and have 3.10 currently living which means that for over three children born around ninety percent are surviving.

Table 4.5 : Percent distribution of ever-married women aged 15-49 years, by number of children ever born and mean number of children ever born and living, according to their present age

Age In yrs	Number of women	Mean children ever born	Mean children living
15-19	27	1	0.8
20-24	113	1.7	1.6
25-29	132	2.9	2.7
30-34	122	3.6	3.4
35-39	80	4	3.7
40-44	41	4.4	4
45-49	44	5.8	5.3
Total	559	3.34	3.1
S.D	-	1.58	1.42

The table shows that the mean number of children ever born increases steadily with age, reaching a high of over five children per woman for the 45-49 age groups. More than one-fifth of the women in the age group of 15-19 years have ever had a child reflecting the past pattern of relatively early marriage and teenage childbearing. The distribution of women aged 45-49 years by number of children ever born is important because these women have nearly completed their childbearing. Thus, the distribution of ever born represents the completed parity distribution for this cohort of women. Results indicate that the older women have higher fertility than the younger women. It is to be recalled that no births have occurred in this age group during the last one year. One-fourth of the women are at parity six, which is higher than the mean number of children ever born of over five (Table 4.5).

Figure 48 Children living in the slum

No. of Children ever-born

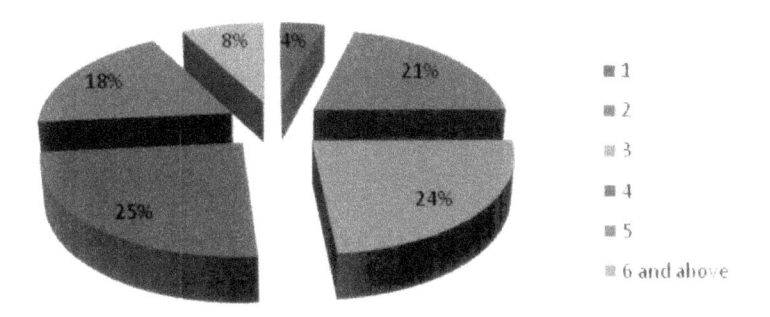

[Pie chart showing: 1: 21%, 2: 24%, 3: 25%, 4: 18%, 5: 8%, 6 and above: 4%]

Figure 49 Graphical representation of the number of children ever born to women

4.6 Reproductive health: Discussion on woman's health is not complete without information on reproductive health and gynaecological problems. Only the (self-perceived) symptoms of the gynaecological problems have been taken into account as there was no scope of clinical testing or monitoring.

4.7 Self-reported symptoms of gynecological problems: Majority of the women included in this study (approximately 70 percent) said that they are suffering from some kind of reproductive health problems. They reported current symptoms suggestive of at least one type of gynecological morbidity. As shown in Table 21, symptoms that may indicate anemia (28 percent) and lower reproductive tract infections (17 percent) were commonly reported, while menstrual problems was also reported by 9.8 percent. But symptoms that may be associated with acute pelvic inflammatory disease (4.6 percent) and urinary tract infections (3.5 percent) were less common. All other symptom categories were reported infrequently: hemorrhoids (2.5 percent), prolapses (2.1 percent) and fistula (1.6 percent).

Table 4.6 :

Percentage of women reporting current symptoms associated with gynecological morbidity, and percentage distribution of duration of specific symptoms:

Symptoms associated with	Reporting symptoms Percent	(N)	Duration of Symptoms (Percent)					Mean duration (in months)
			<3	4-6 months	7-12 months	13+ months	Total	
Anemia	28.2	(158)	22.9	16.4	22.1	36.6	100.0	17.4
Menstrual problems	9.8	(55)	20.1	22.1	15.2	42.6	100.0	20.8
Acute pelvic Inflammatory disease	4.6	(26)	19.3	11.2	23.5	46.0	100.0	23.4
Hemorrhoids	2.5	(14)	36.5	15.9	15.9	31.7	100.0	16.4
Lower reproductive tract Infections	17.1	(96)	15.7	14.7	17.3	52.3	100.0	26.5
Urinary tract Infections	3.5	(20)	35.2	18.5	9.3	37.0	100.0	24.4
Prolapse	2.1	(12)	53.3	13.4	13.4	19.9	100.0	11.9
Fistula	1.6	(9)	22.3	11.1	44.4	22.2	100.0	14.9

4.7.1. Duration of the Symptoms: From the above table it is found that most of the symptoms of the reproductive morbidity among the studied population lasted between less than three months to one year. However a large proportion of these women, ranging from 20 percent to about 50 percent, reported their symptoms to have lasted for more than one year. The mean durations of specific symptoms range between 12 months for symptoms associated with prolapse and 26 months for white/colored vaginal discharge whereas the problems of anemia and lower reproductive tract infections persisted for longer time periods.

It is to be mentioned here that these estimated durations should be interpreted cautiously, because morbid episodes of short durations will be under-represented in any analysis of current perceived morbidity due to ignorance and lack of health awareness among the studied population.

Figure 50 A slum women who was suffering from fistula

4.8 Child care during mother's illness:

If the mother is suffering from illness or is absent for a short duration of time during hospital stay, then in the absence of the mother the child needs to be taken care of. In the studied population it has been found that in absence of the mother mostly it is the older siblings that perform this role.

Table 4.7 : Percent distribution of individuals taking care of the child during mother's illness

		Child care during mother's illness			
		Frequency	Percent	Valid Percent	Cumulative Percent
Valid	Father	9	4.1	4.1	4.1
	Elder Siblings	130	58.8	58.8	62.9
	Grandparents	70	31.7	31.7	94.6
	Neighbors	12	5.4	5.4	100.0
	Total	221	100.0	100.0	

It is interesting to note that in the slums, if the mother is not present at home, it is generally the elder siblings who take care of the infants (59 %), followed by grandparents (32%) and seldom by father (4%) or the neighbors (5%).

Thus it may be said that bio-social factors such as woman's age, educational level, age of menarche, age at marriage, age at first child birth all have important effect on fertility. Urbanization usually leads to modernization and more development, higher literacy, awareness about health care, more contraceptive use, low fertility and a higher living standard, but in the Kolkata slum population, may be mostly due to economic deprivation these things are non-existent.

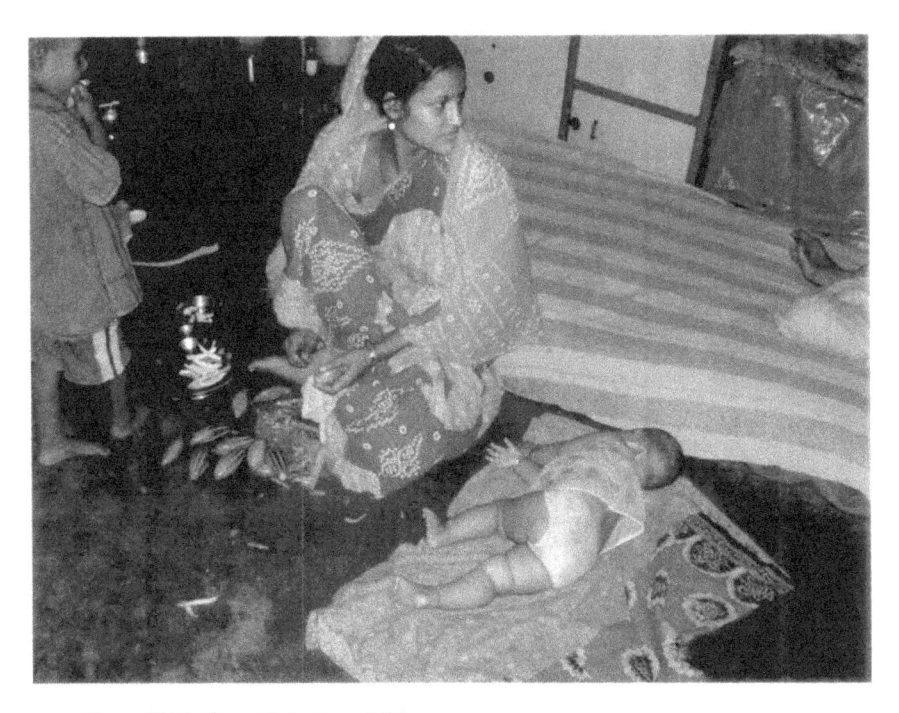

Figure 51 Mother with her two children

Chapter 5

Women's health in slums

Health status of the women in the slums of Kolkata has been accessed by studying 559 ever-married women's concepts regarding family planning, its current usage and unmet needs; ante-natal care (ANC); delivery and post natal care; and awareness in mothers regarding AIDS, child immunization and breastfeeding practices.

5.1 Family planning: Use of contraceptives

Family planning is a very crucial issue in any population by controlling fertility. Family planning through contraception aims to achieve two main objectives; firstly to have only the desired number of children and secondly to have these children by proper spacing of pregnancies. Among the slum dwellers it has been observed, despite having knowledge about family planning and the various means of birth-control, very meager amount is interested and use such measures (34%) and majority (66%) does not adhere to such usage.

Table 5.1: Frequency and percentage of women adopting various methods of family planning through contraceptives

		Usage of contraceptives			
		Frequency	Percent	Valid Percent	Cumulative Percent
Valid	Yes	192	34.3	34.3	34.3
	No	367	65.7	65.7	100.0
	Total	559	100.0	100.0	

Usage of Contraceptives

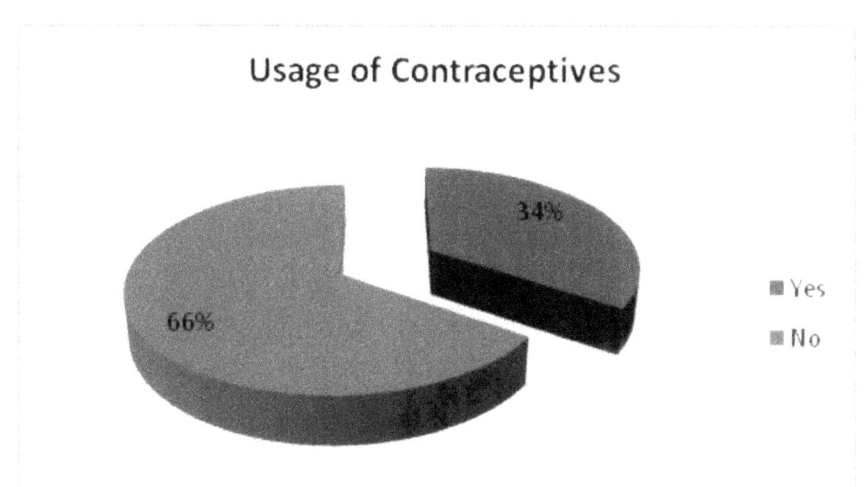

Figure 52 Graphical representation of women using contraceptives for family planning

Among those who use contraceptives, majority opt for oral contraceptive pills (16% out of 34%), followed by condoms (8%) and traditional methods (7%) such as, abstinence, safe period, lactational amenorrhea. Some women also opt for ligation or female sterilization which is a permanent method for pregnancy prevention.

Table 5.2: Frequency and percentage distribution of women using different methods of family planning

	Different Methods of contraceptives used				
		Frequency	Percent	Valid Percent	Cumulative Percent
Valid	Oral Contraceptive Pills	90	16.1	46.9	46.9
	Condoms	47	8.4	24.5	71.4
	Vasectomy	7	1.3	5.2	76.6
	Ultra-Uterine Contraceptive Devices	2	.4	1.0	77.6
	Ligation	10	1.8	3.6	81.3
	Traditional Methods	36	6.4	18.8	100.0
	Total	192	34.3	100.0	
	Did not respond	367	65.7		
Total		559	100.0		

Methods of usage of contraceptives

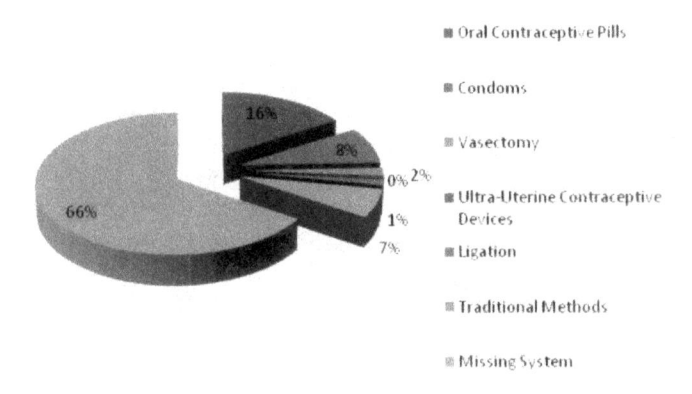

Figure 53 Graphical representation of different methods of family planning practices

Rest of the population, who do not adopt birth control measures give reasons such as, desires for more children (20%), desire for son— if the previous child is a daughter (26%), family pressure (25%), lack of motivation (19%) and other reasons such as, health factors (5%) and lack of knowledge (5%).

Table 5.3: Frequency and percentage distribution of various reasons for not adopting birth control measures

	Reasons of Non-adoption of birth control measures				
		Frequency	Percent	Valid Percent	Cumulative Percent
Valid	More child demand factors	72	12.9	19.6	19.6
	Lack of motivation	70	12.5	19.1	38.7
	Health factors	20	3.6	5.4	44.1
	Wanted son	95	17.0	25.9	70.0
	Family Pressure	90	16.1	24.5	94.6
	Lack of knowledge	20	3.6	5.4	100.0
	Total	367	65.7	100.0	
	Did not respond	192	34.3		
Total		559	100.0		

Reasons for non-adoption of Birth Control Measures

- More child demand factors: 20%
- Lack of motivation: 19%
- Health factors: 5%
- Wanted son: 5%
- Family Pressure: 26%
- Lack of knowledge: 25%

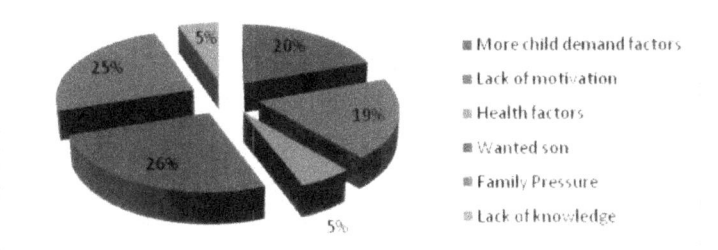

Figure 54 Graphical representation of various reasons owing to which women ignore birth control measures.

5.2 Maternal Health Care

From time to time, health workers have visited the slum areas, to educate and make aware the people, especially women regarding health issues, gynecological problems, child's health, etc. 55% of the women respondents agreed to receive such visits while 45% denied, stating that there are seldom such visits made by health officers.

Table 5.4: Frequency and distribution of home visits made by health or family planning workers in these slums

Table 5.4 Home visit made by a health or family planning workers			Frequency	Percent	Valid Percent	Cumulative Percent
Valid	Yes		307	54.9	54.9	54.9
	No		252	45.1	45.1	100.0
	Total		559	100.0	100.0	

Home visit by a health or family planning workers

- 45%
- 55%
- Yes
- No

Figure 55 Graphical representation of home visits made by health or family planning workers

5.2.1 Antenatal Care (ANC): It is a crucial aspect of maternal health. Under antenatal care, pregnancy complication signs during pregnancy, delivery and postnatal care and related issues are monitored closely. Ideally, for normal pregnancies, once the pregnancy is confirmed, women go for antenatal check-ups at a regular interval of four weeks during first seven months, then every two weeks until last month and weekly thereafter. As per Maternal and Child Health programmes, a pregnant woman should receive two doses of tetanus toxoid vaccine, hundred tablets of iron and folic acid or syrup, and at least three antenatal check-ups. In the slums, about 75 percent of the mothers have received antenatal check-ups (Table 5.5). Of all those who received ante-natal care, all of them have received antenatal check-ups in health institutions indicating that health institutions are accessible to slum women in the Kolkata Municipal Corporation area. For those who did not receive ante-natal care (ANC), 71.5 percent felt that it is unnecessary unless there is a complication. For 12.5 percent woman, check-ups are too costly. And 8.9 percent mothers said that their families did not allow them to get antenatal check-ups or they did not have time to go for antenatal check-ups (Table 5.6). This indicates that there are substantial population who need to be aware about the availability and benefits of these reproductive health services.

Table 5.5 : Percentage of live births (during the four-year period prior to the study), by whether the mother received antenatal check-ups and if not, then reasons for not receiving antenatal check-ups

Antenatal check-ups	Number	Percent
Received	165	74.7
Not received	56	25.3
Total	221	100.0
Reasons for not Receiving Any ANC	No.	%
Not necessary	40	71.5
No time to go	5	8.9
Not permitted by family	4	7.1
Cost too much	7	12.5
Total	56	100.0

Table 5.6 : Percentage of live births (during the four-year period prior to the study), by number of antenatal checkup visits and, by the stage of pregnancy at the time of first visit

ANC visits / months pregnant	Number	Percent
Number of ANC visits		
1-2 visits	37	22.4
3 visits	68	41.2
4 or more visits	60	36.4
Total	165	100.0
Median		3
Months Pregnant at the Time of First ANC Visits		
First trimester	57	34.5
Second trimester	98	59.4
Third trimester	10	6.1
Total	165	100.0
Median	4 months (Second trimester)	

In the slums 77.6 percent of the mothers received at least three antenatal check-ups (Table 6.5. The median number of check-ups is 3 visits. Among mothers who received antenatal care, slightly over 34 percent have received first antenatal check-up in the first trimester of pregnancy (Table 6.6). While about sixty percent have received first antenatal check-up in the second trimester, the median timing of the first antenatal checkup among the slum women of KMC is 4 months i.e., during second trimester of pregnancy. This is in accordance to the guidelines given by the Ministry of Health and Family Welfare, GOI, that there should be at least three antenatal care visits by the women and that first check-up should take place at least during the second trimester of pregnancy.

5.3. Place of Delivery: A significant proportion of neo-natal deaths can be attributed to the poor birth practices. 71.5 per cent of child-births in the slums have took place in their own home while over one-fourth (27.1 per cent) have took place in health facilities (Table 6.7 and 6.8). Out of the births in health facilities, only small proportion has taken place in private medical institutions (0.9 per cent) and 26.2 per cent in public health facilities. Institutional deliveries are more common for births to mother aged 15 -34 years than for mothers aged 35+. They are also more common for first births (32.0 per cent) than for later births.

Table- 5.7: Distribution of live births (during the four-year period prior to the study), by mother's education and place of delivery

Characteristics	Place of delivery				Total
MOTHER'S EDUCATION	Public hospitals institutions	Private medical	Home	Public places/others	Number of live births
Illiterate/ Cannot Sign	2(4.5)	0(0.0)	42(93.3)	1(2.2)	45(100.0)
Can Sign	9(10.8)	0(0.0)	72(86.8)	2(2.4)	83(100.0)
Primary	25(36.7)	0(0.0)	43(63.3)	0(0.0)	68(100.0)
Secondary	19(95.0)	0(0.0)	1(5.0)	0(0.0)	20(100.0)
Higher Secondary	0(0.0)	1(100.0)	0(0.0)	0(0.0)	1(100.0)
Graduation & Above	3(75.0)	1(25.0)	0(0.0)	0(0.0)	4(100.0)
Total	58(26.2)	2(0.9)	158(71.5)	3(1.4)	221(100.0)

From the table 5.7 it can be said that the likelihood of institutional delivery increases with mother's education indicating that awareness about the benefits of professional medical care during pregnancy and delivery is more among the women with higher education (Table 5.7).

Table 5.8 : Distribution of live births (during the four-year period prior to the study), By place of delivery and mother's age at birth of first child

Characteristics	Public hospitals institutions	Private medical	Home	Public places/ Others	Number of live births
Mother's age (in yrs) at childbirth		PLACE OF DELIVERY			
15-19	10(55.5)	1(5.6)	7(38.9)	-	18(100.0)
20-34	47(23.73)	1(0.51)	148 (74.75)	2(1.01)	198(100.0)
35+	1(20.0)	0(0.0)	3(60.0)	1(20.0)	5(100.0)
Total	58(26.2)	2(0.9)	158(71.5)	3(1.4)	221(100.0)

Percentage distribution of live births

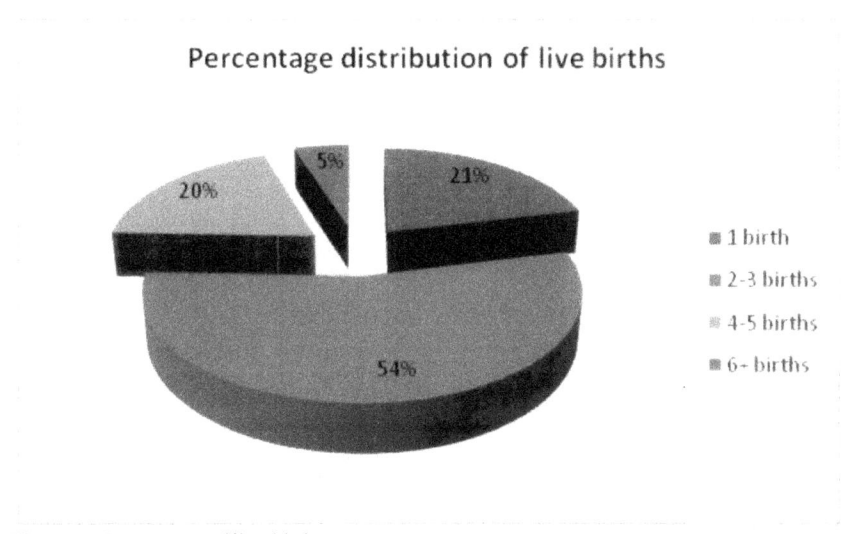

- 1 birth: 21%
- 2-3 births: 54%
- 4-5 births: 20%
- 6+ births: 5%

Figure 56 Percentage of live births.

Table- 5.9 : Distribution of live births (during the four-year period prior to the study), by place of delivery and Birth Order

Characteristics	Place of delivery				Total
BIRTH ORDER	Public hospitals	Private medical institutions	Home	Public places/others	Number of live births
1	14(29.9)	1(2.1)	31(65.9)	1(2.1)	47(100.0)
2-3	32(26.7)	1(0.9)	85(70.8)	2(1.6)	120(100.0)
4-5	8(18.6)	-	35(81.4)	-	43(100.0)
6+	4(36.4)	-	7(63.6)	-	11(100.0)
Total	58(26.2)	2(0.9)	158(71.5)	3(1.4)	221(100.0)

Table- 5.10 : Distribution of live births (during the four-year period prior to the study), by place of delivery and Antenatal Care (ANC) received

Characteristics	Place of delivery				Total
ANTENATAL CARE VISITS	Public hospitals	Private medical institutions	Home	Public places/others	Number of live births
None	-	-	54(96.4)	2(3.6)	56(100.0)
1-2 Visits	3(8.1)	-	33(89.2)	1(2.7)	37(100.0)
3 Visits	22(32.4)	-	46(67.6)	-	68(100.0)
4 +	33(55.0)	2(3.4)	25(41.6)	-	60(100.0)
Total	58(26.2)	2(0.9)	158(71.5)	3(1.4)	221(100.0)

Thus it can be said that the number of children born and living is affected by several factors like delivery place, mother's education, birth order and antenatal care received by the mother (Tables 5.9 and 5.10).

Table 5.11 : Frequency and percentage of respondents visiting public hospitals

		Frequency	Percent	Valid Percent	Cumulative Percent
Valid	Yes	300	53.7	53.7	53.7
	No	259	46.3	46.3	100.0
	Total	559	100.0	100.0	

The slum women, those who seek medical care, mostly visit the public hospitals in case of any severe health related problems. But in case of less severe illness, most of them opt for treatment at home, mostly adhering to herbal or faith healing. Hence it can be summed up that, the data related to pregnancy, delivery, ante and post natal care and other health practices of the women respondents project a miserable condition. The analyses shows that mostly due to lack of proper education and awareness and lack of basic amenities, most of them suffer from various types of reproductive and general illness, for prolonged time periods.

Visit to any public hospitals

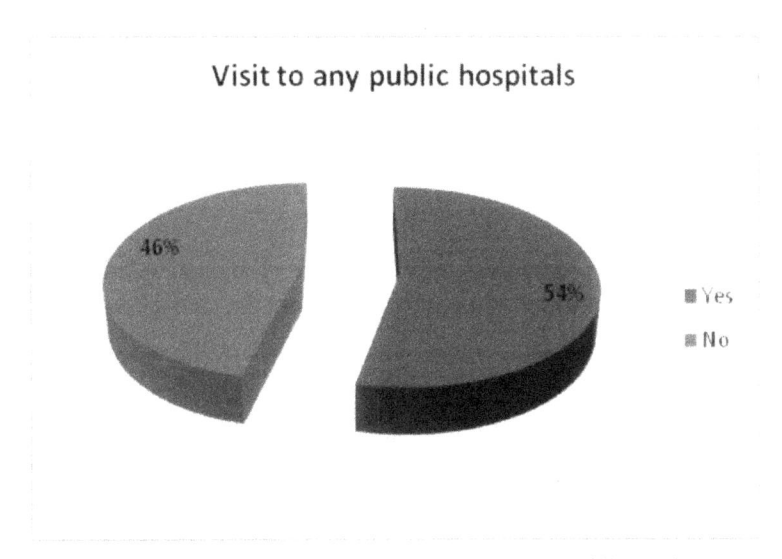

Figure 57 Graphical representation of respondent's visit to any public hospitals

5.4 Awareness about AIDS, healthy pregnancy and other health –related concepts among the women studied

It has been observed from the data analyses of the indicators of the women dwelling in the four slums of Kolkata that, majority of the women are illiterate, so this section aims to analyze their perception of health and diseases these respondents have and its effect on their health practices. In the previous chapter it was found that most of the women had their menarche during the age of 13 to 16 years, and when asked if they had prior knowledge of such natural occurrence, 97.9% agreed while only 2.1% said they had no such knowledge. The source of information regarding menstruation, AIDS and that of pregnancy has been credited to the media (53.7%) — television, primarily and different kinds of printed advertisements. Peer groups also played a significant source in imparting such knowledge (32%), while mother (8.9%) and books (5.4%) are not considered as source of attaining knowledge about significant changes one's body undergoes. Those who were unaware of these were mostly the respondents who had their menarche at a very young age, within 10-11 years.

Table 5.12 : Frequency and percentage distribution of women having prior information about menstruation and childbirth

		\multicolumn{4}{c	}{Any prior information about menstruation, or childbirth}
		Frequency	Percent	Valid Percent	Cumulative Percent
Valid	Yes	547	97.9	97.9	97.9
	No	12	2.1	2.1	100.0
	Total	559	100.0	100.0	

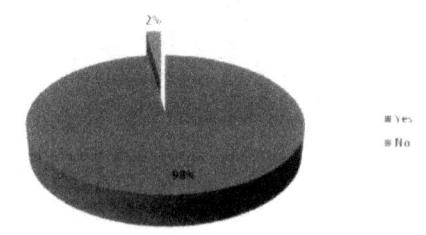

Figure 58 Graphical representation of women having prior information about menstruation and childbirth

Table 5.13 : Frequency and percentage distribution of source of information about menstruation, AIDS, among these women.

Table 5.13 Source of information about onset of menstruation, and AIDS awareness

		Frequency	Percent	Valid Percent	Cumulative Percent
Valid	Mother	50	8.9	8.9	8.9
	Media	300	53.7	53.7	62.6
	Book	30	5.4	5.4	68.0
	Peer groups	179	32.0	32.0	100.0
	Total	559	100.0	100.0	

Source of Information about menstruation

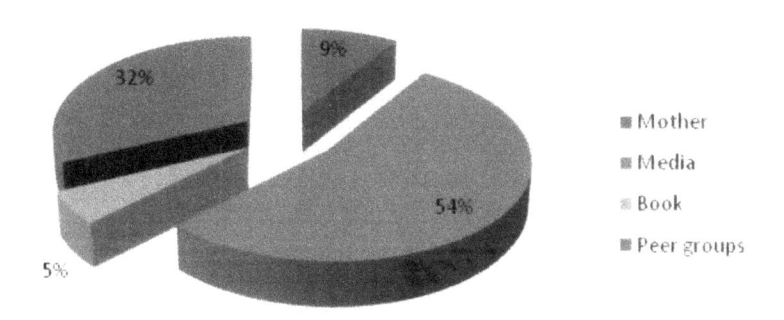

Figure 59 Graphical representation of source of information about menstruation, AIDS, among these women

When enquired about the first reaction at the onset of menstruation or news of first pregnancy the responses are within varying range from 'pleasure' (34.9%) to 'surprise' (25%), and fear (17.9%) to 'feeling ashamed' (19.7%). The reaction of pleasure and surprise though were mostly related to news of first pregnancy and feeling ashamed with that of menstruation. Very few were 'shocked' (1.8%) and had 'no reactions' at all (0.7%).

Table 5.14 : Frequency and percentage distribution of women's reaction on the initial onset of menstruation and news of pregnancy

Initial reactions at the onset of menstruation, news of first pregnancy					
		Frequency	Percent	Valid Percent	Cumulative Percent
Valid	Shock	10	1.8	1.8	1.8
	Pleasure	195	34.9	34.9	36.7
	Surprise	140	25.0	25.0	61.7
	No reaction	4	0.7	0.7	62.4
	Feared	100	17.9	17.9	80.3
	Felt ashamed	110	19.7	19.7	100.0
	Total	559	100.0	100.0	

First reaction at the onset of menstruation/news of first pregnancy

- Shock 2%
- Pleasure 35%
- Surprise 25%
- No reaction 1%
- Feared 18%
- Felt ashamed 19%

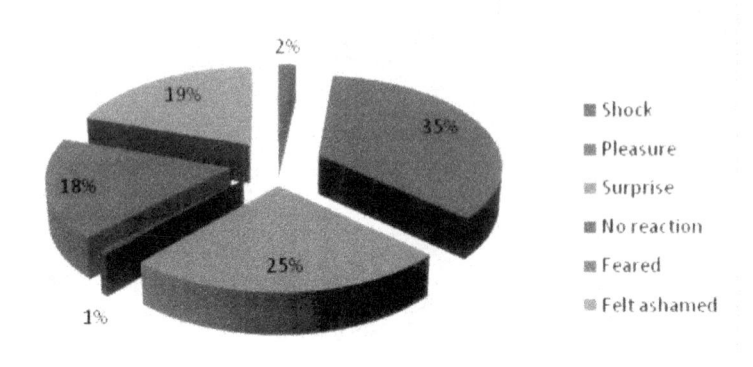

Figure 60 Graphical representation of women's reaction on the initial onset of menstruation and news of pregnancy

Table 5.15 : Frequency and percentage distribution of women agreeing/disagreeing to rituals performed after attending menarche, pregnancy

	Any specific rituals performed after attending menarche, pregnancy
		Frequency	Percent Percent	Valid Percent	Cumulative
Valid	No	559	100.0	100.0	100.0

Table 5.16 : Frequency and percentage distribution of women continuing their work during illness and pregnancy

	**CONTINUATION OF WORK DURING PREGNENCY**
		Frequency	Percent	Valid Percent	Cumulative Percent
Valid	Yes	500	89.4	89.4	89.4
	No	59	10.6	10.6	100.0
	Total	559	100.0	100.0	

During interviews, majority of the women respondents answered that they continue with their job without taking any long leaves during pregnancy or illness due to their poor economic conditions and temporary nature of work. Most of the respondents fear losing job if leaves are taken. Leaves are only taken during one month prior to delivery and two months post-delivery. Maternity leave of three months or beyond is s considered as a luxury which most of them could not afford.

Continuation of work during pregnancy/illness

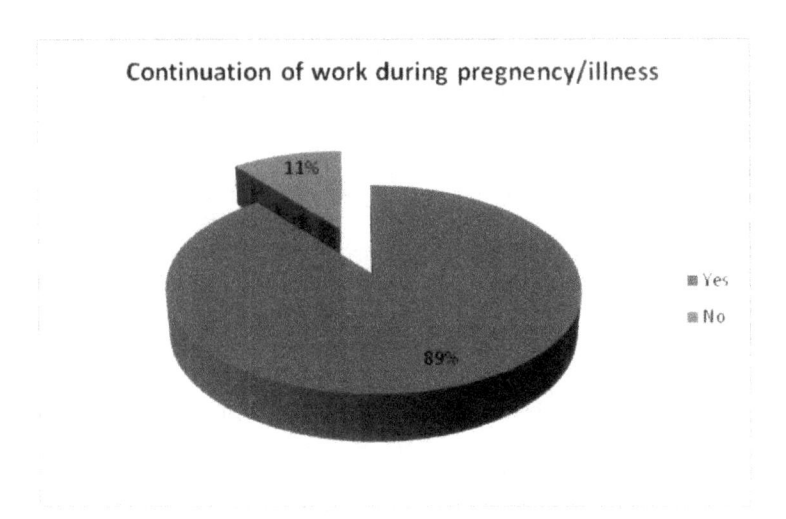

Figure 61 Graphical representation of women continuing their work during illness and pregnancy

5.4.1 AIDS awareness among the studied population:

When enquired about AIDS awareness, 69.2% women said to have the knowledge of AIDS as well as the reasons of its spread, while 30.8% answered that they do not have clear concepts regarding the syndrome. Among those who have the knowledge, unfortunately do not do anything to prevent the disease (53.7%). Although some 'avoid contact with multiple partners' (26.8%), while few 'use condoms' (10.7%) and they also make sure of 'avoiding used needles' at health centers (8.8%).

Table 5.17 : Frequency and percentage of women having knowledge of AIDS

Awareness about AIDS					
		Frequency	Percent	Valid Percent	Cumulative Percent
Valid	Yes	387	69.2	69.2	69.2
	No	172	30.8	30.8	100.0
	Total	559	100.0	100.0	

Knowledge of concept of AIDS

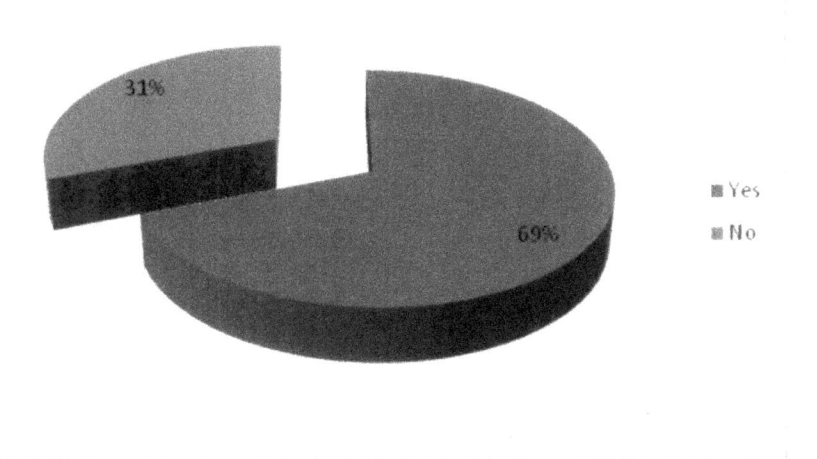

- 31% No
- 69% Yes

Figure 62 Graphical representation of AIDS awareness among women

Table 5.18 : Frequency and percentage distribution of women believing in different ways of prevention of AIDS

	Awareness of the Ways to prevent AIDS among the studied population				
		Frequency	Percent	Valid Percent	Cumulative Percent
Valid	Use condoms	60	10.7	10.7	10.7
	Make sure that used needles are not used at hospitals	49	8.8	8.8	19.5
	Avoid contact with multiple partners	150	26.8	26.8	46.3
	Don't do anything	300	53.7	53.7	100.0
	Total	559	100.0	100.0	

Ways to prevent AIDS

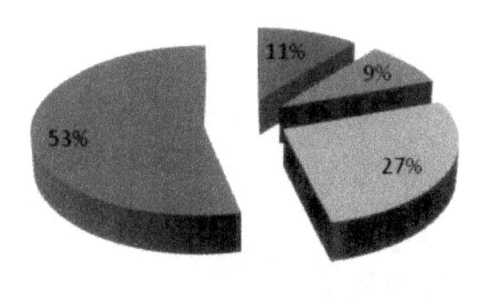

- Use condoms — 53%
- Make sure that used needles are not used at hospitals — 11%
- Avoid contact with multiple partners — 27%
- Don t do anything — 9%

Figure 63 Graphical representation of women believing in different ways of prevention of AIDS

5.4.2 'Safe' and 'Risky' (sexual) behaviors : Although in practice, the women respondents do not take up any method to prevent AIDS and it they mostly depend on their spouses to take decisions, yet their perceptions regarding 'safe' and 'risky' behaviors in preventing AIDS is somewhat clear. 71% believe 'having single partners' is among the safe behavior and 29% believe in the 'use of condoms' as 'safe'. Regarding risky behaviors — 89.6% believe that 'unprotected sex', and 10.4% believe that 'unsterilized needle' with HIV infections (5.7%) and 'blood transfusions' (4.7%) are among risky behaviors.

Table 5.19 : Frequency and percentage distribution of women's perception of 'safe' behaviors

		Frequency	Percent	Valid Percent	Cumulative Percent
Valid	Use of condoms	162	29.0	29.0	29.0
	Single partners	397	71.0	71.0	100.0
	Total	559	100.0	100.0	

Concept of 'safe' behaviors

- Use of condoms: 29%
- Single partner: 71%

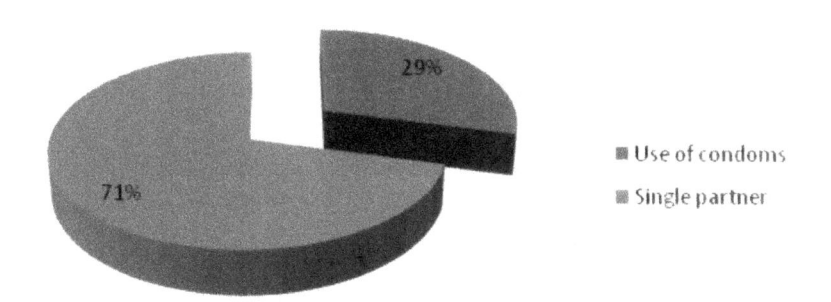

Figure 64 Graphical representation of women's perception of 'safe' behaviors

Table 5.20 : Frequency and percentage distribution of women's perception of 'risky' behaviors

		Frequency	Percent	Valid Percent	Cumulative Percent
Valid	Unprotected sex	501	89.6	89.6	89.6
	Injecting of unsterilized needles infected with HIV	32	5.7	5.7	95.3
	Recipients of blood transfusions	26	4.7	4.7	100.0
	Total	559	100.0	100.0	

Figure 65 Graphical representation of women's perception of 'risky' behaviors

Concept of 'risky' behaviors

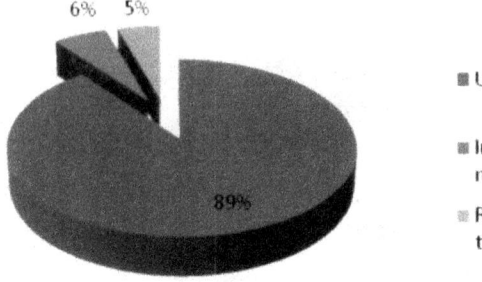

- Unprotected sex — 89%
- Injecting of unsterilized needles infected with HIV — 6%
- Recipents of blood transfusions — 5%

5.5 Alternative healthcare and medical treatments:

Women in the studied slums have been adopting various indigenous methods and alternative methods of treatments. Complementary and Alternative healthcare and Medical practices (CAM) is a group of diverse medical and health care systems, practices, and products that are not presently considered to be part of conventional medicine. The list of practices that are considered as CAM may change continually. Complementary medicine refers to therapies that complement traditional western (or allopathic) medicine and is used together with conventional medicine, and alternative medicine is used in place of conventional medicine. The basic philosophy of complementary and alternative medicine includes holistic care, which focuses on treating a human being as a whole person.

Examples of complementary and alternative medicine healing systems include Ayurveda, which originated in India. Homeopathy uses minute doses of a substance that causes symptoms to stimulate the body's self-healing response. Naturopathy focuses on non-invasive treatments to help the body do its own healing. All these systems are based on the belief that one's body has the power to heal itself. Faith healing often involves marshalling multiple techniques that involve the mind, body and spirit. Treatment is often individualized and dependent on the presenting symptoms. The alternative systems of medicines like Ayurveda, Siddha, Unani and Homeopathy are all licenced by the Indian government and most people use these alternative treatments for recurring problems. It was found that women in general are more likely to use alternative medical treatments than men.

The reasons and frequency of using CAM among the slum women have been mentioned below.

Table 5.21 : Frequency and percentage distribution of women taking alternative medical treatment in the last five years

		Frequency	Percent	Valid Percent	Cumulative Percent
Valid	Yes	214	38.3	38.3	38.3
	No	345	61.7	61.7	100.0
	Total	559	100.0	100.0	

Usage of alternative medical treatment

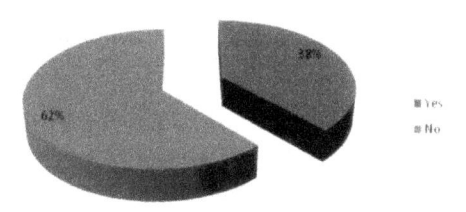

Figure 66 Graphical representation of women taking alternative medical treatment in the last five years

Table 5.22: Frequency and percentage distribution of women citing various reasons for taking alternative medical treatment in the last five years

	Reasons for using alternative medical treatment				
		Frequency	Percent	Valid Percent	Cumulative Percent
Valid	Previous medicine was not effective	42	7.5	19.6	19.6
	Alternative medicine was cheap	87	15.6	40.7	60.3
	It was recommended by my family and friends	85	15.2	39.7	100.0
	Totaal	214	38.3	100.0	
	Did not respond	345	61.7		
	Total	559	100.0		

Reason behing using alternative medical treatment

- Previous medicine was not effective — 19%
- Alternative medicine was cheap — 41%
- It was recommended by my family and friends — 40%

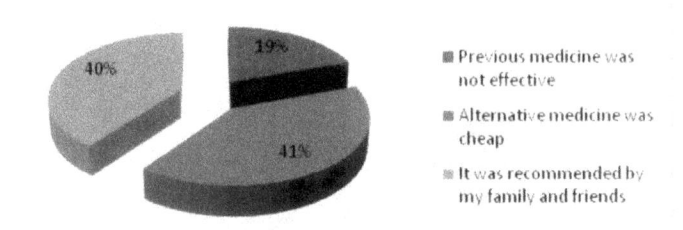

Figure 67 Graphical representation of women taking alternative medical treatment in the last five years

Mostly living in impoverished conditions, majority of the population are unable to afford costly conventional medical treatment, thereby mostly visiting public or government hospitals. Due to this non affordability along with some traditional and orthodox belief and perceptions, 38.3% resorted to alternative medical treatment, like faith healing (17.2%), herbalism (9.8%), Homeopathy (7.5%) and Ayurveda (3.8%). The reasons behind such alternative treatment has been cited as, alternative medicines were cheap (15.6%), recommended by family or friends (15.2%) or ineffectiveness of previous medicines (7.5%). In some instances, more than 60% cases, alternative treatments were used alongside conventional treatments and sometimes even in combination.

Table 5.23: Frequency and percentage distribution of different types of alternative medical treatments

		Frequency	Percent	Valid Percent	Cumulative Percent
Valid	Homeopathy	42	7.5	19.6	19.6
	Herbalism	55	9.8	25.7	45.3
	Faith healing	96	17.2	44.9	90.2
	Ayurveda	21	3.8	9.8	100.0
	Total	214	38.3	100.0	
	Combination of all types	345	61.7		
	Total	559	100.0		

Types of alternate medicine used

Different types of alternative medical treatment

- Homeopathy 19%
- Herbalism 26%
- faith healing 10%
- Ayurveda 45%

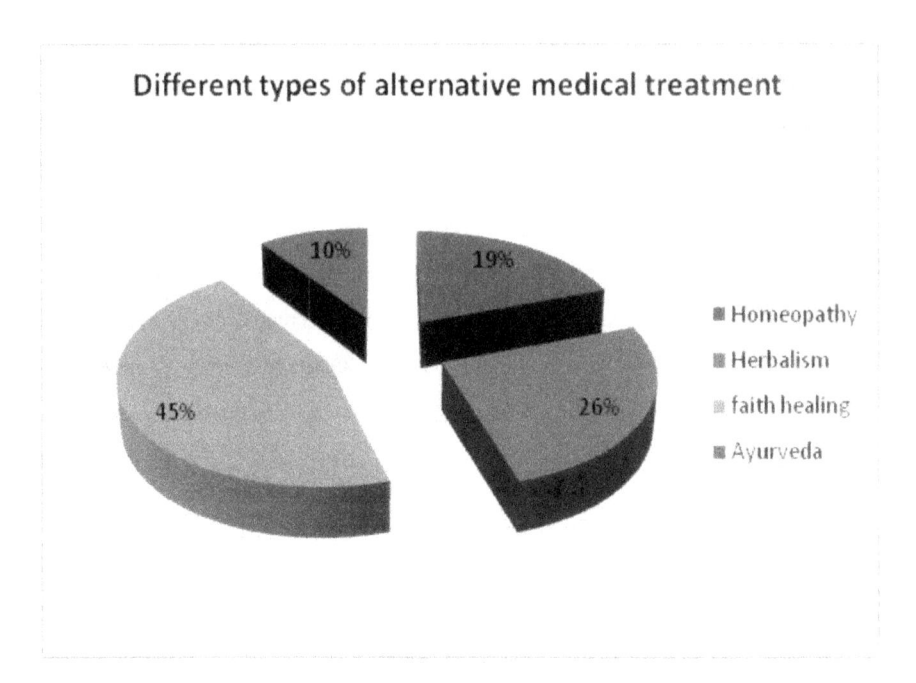

Figure 68 Graphical representation of alternative medical treatments used by women in the study population

Thus, this chapter gives a holistic view on the overall health conditions; occurrence of diseases and treatments availed by the women in the slums of Kolkata.

Chapter 6

Child Health and Diseases in Slums

Child health is a major cause for concern in developing countries like India. It has been found that, though the rural areas have higher mortality rate than the urban areas, the slums have registered the highest mortality rate. One of the preventive measures that are being implemented is the introduction of immunization schedule system. The parental level of education (especially the mothers), the number of times they attend the health centres, immunization and household income are the key factors influencing the health of the children. In this chapter the main themes of child health which have been taken into account are: (1) Child Immunization (2) Childhood Diseases and their treatment (3) Breast Feeding Practices.

6.1 Child Immunization

The current population of India is approximately 1.21 billion; children below six years make up 13% of it. About 7.6 million children are living in slums in India, every eighth urban children in India in the age-group of 0 - 6 years lives in slums. It is important to note that approximately 26 million children in India are born each year, of which twelve thousand die below five years, annually (Patel et al., 2014). It is shocking to find that 81% of these deaths happen before the child reaches one year (Piaget, 2013). 57 % die within their first month. The Fourth Millennium Development Goal in 2000 by the World Health Organisation aims to reduce child and infant mortality rate by two-thirds. India was among the 189 nations who came together and came up with Millennium Development Goals. Despite many efforts ,the current estimates show that more than 44 developing countries have less than 20% chance of achieving this goal (Reddy, Pradhan, Ghosh, & Khan, 2012).

A recent clinical study focussing on immunization showed that currently, more than 34 million children have not been immunized against measles (Sreedhar, 2013). The Government of India has been pushing for Immunization against various diseases like diphtheria, tetanus, measles, pertussis, polio and typhoid. Part of the immunization is done soon after the child has been born, and the rest are spread up to the age of 2 years.

Table 6.1: Distribution of child population immunized in the slum

Name of vaccine		Number of children immunized	Percent
	DPT	172	78.0
	BCG	176	80.0
	Measles	161	73.8
	Polio	214	97.9
Total number of children present between (0-4)years of age		221	100.0

Table 6.1 shows that in the slums almost 97.9 % of the children were administered the polio vaccine, 78% were given DPT and 80% BCG. Measles immunization was relatively lesser, only 73.8% among the study population. Of the population which chose to not immunize their child against these diseases, different parents have given various reasons as to why their children have not been immunized. Most of them claim that they were not fully aware that the children needed the vaccination; others claimed that they had lesser access to a medical facility; while others said the cost of giving vaccine caused hindrance.

Figure 69 Children in the slum

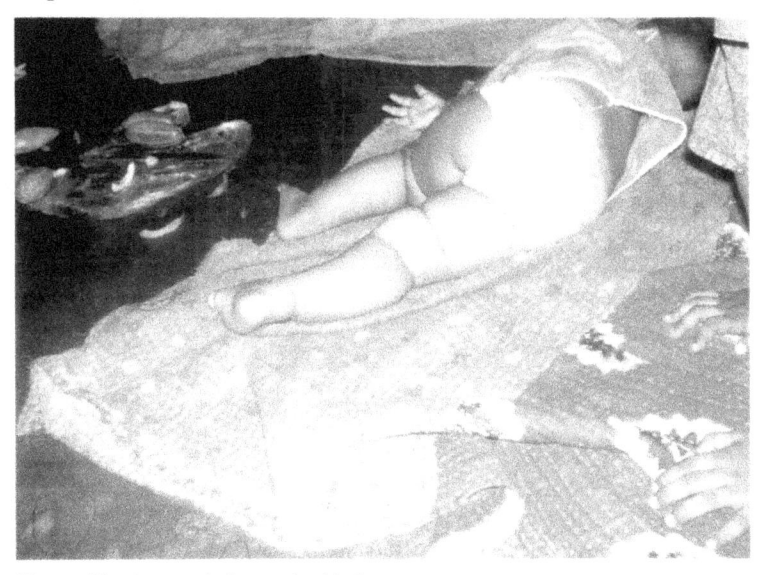

Figure 70 A recently immunised baby

A clinical study was conducted in 2010 in the slums where one-third of the children below the age of 3 years had not received any vaccination. Among the people who were interviewed, 33% of parents had not taken their children for immunization and answered that they were unaware of the need for immunization.

Most of the parents who gave this reason had a low-level education. 13.1 % of the mother whose children had not received immunization said that they did not know the time and place when the immunization was supposed to given. 7.7 % said that time and place was inconvenient for them, and most of those mothers who gave this reason were working and returned to their workplace soon after birth. 5.3% said that they feared the side effects that might be caused by the immunization, which might be because of the myths and misconceptions that they have heard. 3.2 % said they had no faith in the immunization system. These mothers may have observed other children who had not survived even after being immunized. 8.3 % said that there were no vaccination medicines at nearby hospitals and clinics. 0. 4% said that they were just tired of the long queues that one has to go through to get just one vaccination. 14.4% feared that their child was too young to get the vaccine. 8.9% said it was due to some family problems that prevented them from their children getting the vaccine. 6.3% had other reasons (Diekema, 2012). The information is represented in a pie chart as shown below:

Reasons for lack of immunization

- unaware of need for immunization
- place time unknown
- place time inconvinient
- fear of side effects
- No faith in immunization
- Vaccine not available
- Long waiting time
- Child too young
- Family problems
- Other reasons

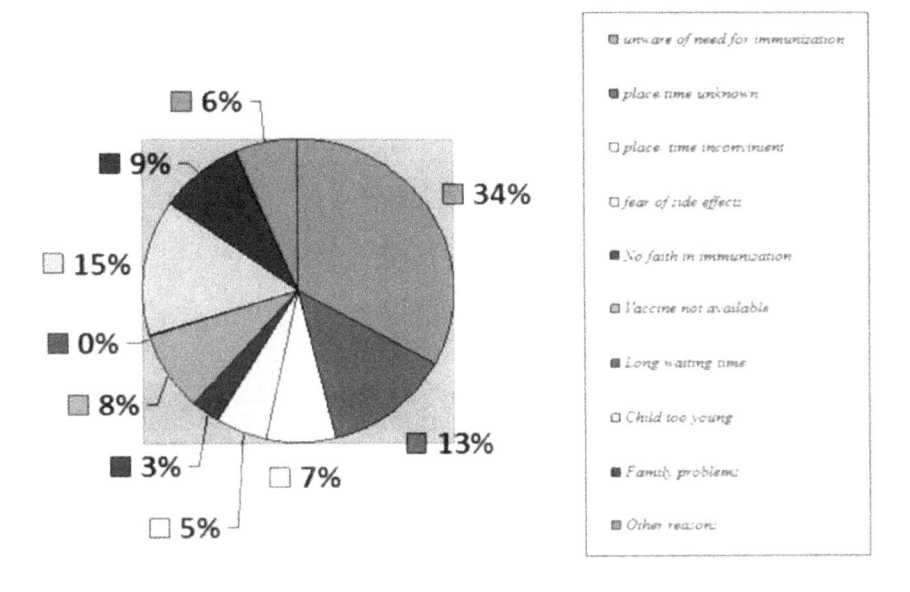

34%, 13%, 7%, 5%, 3%, 8%, 0%, 15%, 9%, 6%

Figure. 71 Showing reasons for not vaccinating

6.2 Childhood Diseases

Prevalence of poor sanitary conditions and ignorance of the slum dwellers in maintaining healthy and unhygienic lifestyle, leads to 61% of children suffering from various diseases such as, diarrhea, fever, cold & cough, malaria etc. in the slum population under study.

Table 6.2: Frequency Distribution of infants and children (aged between 0-4 years) suffering from various diseases, in past one year in the study population

		Frequency	Percent	Valid Percent	Cumulative Percent
Valid	No	86	39.0	39.0	39.0
	Yes	135	61.0	61.0	100.0
	Total	221	100.0	100.0	

Infants (aged 0-12 months) and children (1-4 yrs.) suffering from disease, in the past 1 year

Child or infant suffering from any disease in the past one year

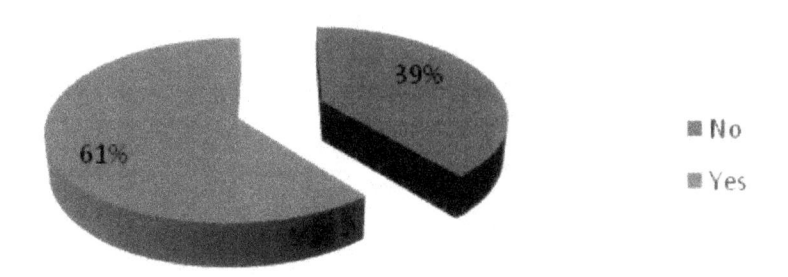

- No: 39%
- Yes: 61%

Figure 72 Graphical representation of children and infants (aged between 0-4 years) suffering from disease in past one year

Nature of disease: infectious, non-infectious, hereditary

■ Non-infectious
■ Infectious

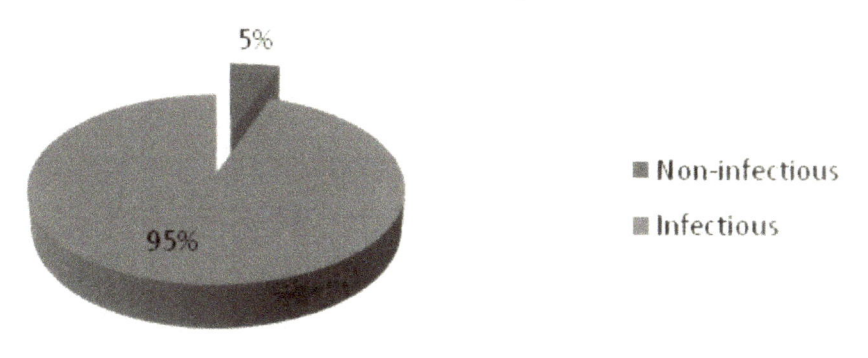

5%
95%

Figure 73 Graphical representation of nature of disease among children

Figure showing that diseases are essentially not hereditary in nature, but are mostly infectious (95%), spreading from the unhygienic and polluted surroundings.

Tables 6.3 and 6.4 provided below shows the different diseases affecting the children (1-4 years) and infants (0-12 months) in the studied slums and the treatments adopted by their families. Following Table 6.3 suggest the varying treatment followed in cases of cold and cough, fever, diarrhea by mothers having different education levels.

Table 6.3: Distribution of children under four years of age, having common ailments like cough (accompanied by short and rapid breathing), fever, and diarrhea during two weeks period prior to study, by selected characteristics

Characteristics	Number of children (%)	Disease affecting children (0-4 yrs.) (in percentage)		
		Cough (ARI)	Influenza	Diarrhea
Total	221(100)	15(6.8)	26(11.8)	44(19.9)
Age of Child (in months)				
0-5	21	19.0	4.8	28.6
6-11	40	10.0	15.0	27.5
12-23	62	8.1	14.5	22.6
24-35	54	1.9	9.3	18.5
36-47	44	2.3	11.4	6.8
Sex of Child				
Males	134	6.7	10.4	20.9
Females	87	6.9	13.8	18.4
Education of Mother				
Illiterate	55	5.5	5.5	32.7
Primary education	62	3.2	14.5	19.4
Secondary education	55	10.9	9.1	18.2

6.3 Child Morbidity and Treatment:

Acute respiratory infections (ARI), primarily pneumonia, diarrhea and low birth weight are the major causes of child morbidity among infants and children in Kolkata slums. Most of the children suffering from infectious or non-infectious diseases are treated in public hospitals

or home. Only in case of severity they are taken to a hospital or a doctor. As the graph below reflects, 75% are treated in public hospitals, 13% at home and only 8% and 4% at private hospitals and nursing homes.

Child taken for treatment

- Public hospital
- Private hospital
- Nursing home
- At home itself

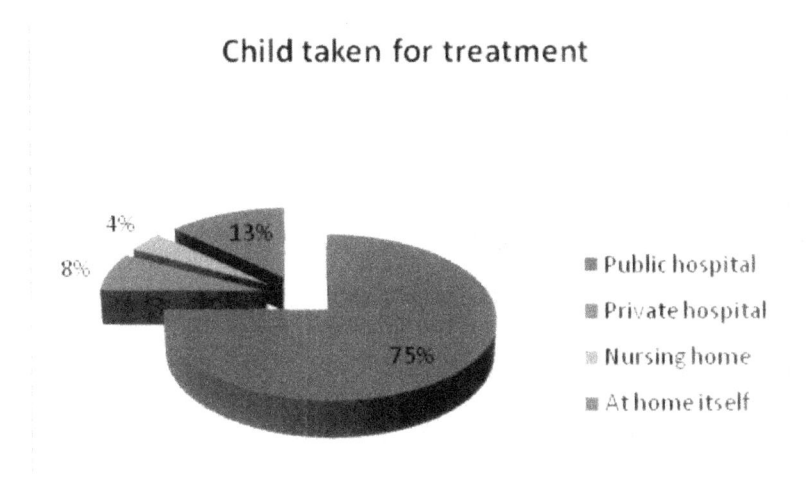

4%
13%
8%
75%

Figure 74 Graphical representation of places of treatment of children

Figure 75 Children "chotus" working in slum shop

Figure 76 A polyclinic in the slum area

Table 6.4: Percent distribution of children under four years of age, having cough accompanied by short and rapid breathing in the past two weeks, by treatment

Characteristics	Total number of child suffering from cough ,rapid breathing	
	Number	Percent
Treatment Availed		
Not treated	2	13.3
Taken to hospital or doctor	13	86.7
Total	15	100.0
If Treated		
Injection	1	6.6
Pills	3	20.0
Syrup	9	60.0
Home remedy	2	13.4

A closer look at the treatment pattern reveals that majority of children who suffered from Acute Respiratory Infection were taken to a health facility (e.g. hospital) or provider (doctor) for treatment (Table 6.4). About 14 percent of the children with ARI did not receive any treatment. Suffering children were most often treated with pills and cough syrup.

Table 6.5: Percent distribution of children under four years of age having fever, flu in the past two weeks, by treatment

Characteristics	Total number of child suffering from fever	
	Number	Percent
Treatment		
Untreated	4	15.4
Taken to hospital or doctor	22	84.6
Total	26	100.00
If Treated		
Injection	5	19.2
Pills or Syrup	19	73.1
Anti-malarial	2	7.7
Home remedy	-	-

Another, major cause of child morbidity is flue, accompanied by fever which in turn accompanies various illnesses importantly with malaria. The incidence of fever, during two weeks was lower than diarrhoea. About twelve percent of the children suffered from fever (Table 6.5). Children aged 6-23 months were somewhat more prone to fever. Fever is also more common in females than males. No consistent relationship is observed between the prevalence of fever and the education of the mother. More than four-fifth of the children with fever were taken to a health facility or provider for treatment (Table 6.5). Majority of children were treated with pills and injections. Anti-malarial medication was give to less than ten percent of the children. Treatment at a health facility or by a health provider was more common for children under two years of age and for male children.

Table 6.6: Percent distribution of children less than four years of age, having diarrhea in the past two weeks, by whether treated or not; sex of the child and mother's education.

Characteristics	Number of children having diarrhoea	Not treated — Taken to doctor or	If treated then — Treated at home hospital	
Age of Child (in months)				
0-11	17	-	82.4	17.6
12-23	14	7.1	78.6	14.3
24-47	13	30.8	53.8	15.4
Gender of Child				
Males	28	7.1	82.1	10.7
Females	16	18.8	56.3	25.0
Education of Mother				
Illiterate	18	16.7	61.1	22.2
Primary education	12	8.3	7.0	16.7
Secondary education	10	10.0	80.0	10.0
Higher Secondary and Above	4	-	100.0	-
Total Percent	**100.0**	**11.4**	**72.7**	**15.9**
Total Number	**44**	**5**	**32**	**7**

It has been found that diarrhoea is the most common of the three conditions examined during the study. One-fifth of the children under four years of age had diarrhea during two weeks prior to study (Table 6.5). The incidence of diarrhoea declines with increasing age.

Children aged 36-47 months are least susceptible to diarrhoea. Diarrhoea is more prevalent among males than females and higher among children of illiterate women. The differentials in the likelihood of taking treatment or medical advice for diarrhoea with respect to mother's education do not reflect a consistent pattern. (Table 6.6). The likelihood of taking the child to the hospital increases with increase in the level of education of the mother. However, less than sixteen percent of the children having diarrhoea were treated at home.

Table 6.7 Percent distribution of children less than four years of age, having diarrhoea in the past two weeks, by age and feeding practices during diarrhoea

Feeding practices among infants (0-11 months) and children (up to 4 years) during diarrhoea		*Age of child (in months)*
Amount of Fluids Given	0-11	0-47*
Same as usual	64.7	56.8
More	23.5	27.3
Less	11.8	15.9
Total percent	100.0	100.0
Number of children with diarrhoea	17	44
Frequency of Breastfeeding		
Same as usual	76.5	73.9
Increased	17.6	17.4
Decreased	5.9	8.7
Total percent	100.0	100.0
Number of children who are still breastfed	17	23
*Includes children who are aged 0-11 months		

Although the likelihood of taking the child to the hospital increases with increase in the level of education of the mother, however, less than sixteen percent of the children having diarrhoea were treated at home. In majority of children the amount of other fluids given was maintained at the same level. About one in every six children with diarrhoea was given less fluid than they received before the diarrhoea began. The percentage of children who were given fewer fluids was less among those who were under one year than those who were older. For majority of children the frequency of breastfeeding was also unchanged. The frequency increased during the diarrhoea in over one-sixth of children and decreased in less than ten percent of children. The frequency of breastfeeding was the same for a larger proportion of children under one year than those who were older. For majority of children the frequency of breastfeeding was unchanged. The frequency increased during the diarrhoea in over one-sixth of children and decreased in less than ten percent of children. The frequency of breastfeeding was the same for a larger proportion of children under one year than those who were older. All of the children aged 0-5 months are fully breastfed while nearly ninety-three percent of the children below one year are breastfed exclusively, remaining are partially breastfed (i.e., received supplements such as other milk like cow's milk, other liquid, or solid or mushy food).

Figure 77 A child in the slum house

6.4 Breastfeeding practices

Breast feeding can have significant effects on child survival and health as well as maternal fertility and health. Reproductive and Child Health Programme, Government of India, recommends that infants should be exclusively breastfed up to six months of age and continued as long as possible for the mother.

All of the children aged 0-5 months in the study population are fully breastfed while 92.5 percent of the children below one year are breastfed exclusively, remaining are partially breastfed (i.e., received supplements such as other milk like cow's milk, other liquid, or solid or mushy food). The proportion of children who are fully breastfed decreases rapidly with age as children are gradually weaned from the breast. Cumulatively 60% infants are breast feed and 40% receive for a very limited time, after which breast feeding is complicated and gradually substituted by other feeding supplements. As the table below reflects, children who are exclusively being breast fed are decreasing with increase in age, while breastfeeding with other supplements have larger amount of infants older than 6 months.

Table 6.8 : Distribution of children under four years of age according to present breastfeeding status by age and sex of the children

Characteristics	Not breastfeeding presently	Exclusively breastfeeding	Breastfeeding with other supplements	Total children
Age of child (in months)				
0-5	--(0.0)	21 (100.0)	--(0.0)	21(100.0)
6-11	--(0.0)	37 (92.5)	3 (7.5)	40(100.0)
12-17	--(0.0)	8 (66.6)	4 (33.4)	12(100.0)
18-23	18 (36.0)	1 (2.0)	31 (62.0)	50(100.0)
24-29	2 (40.0)	--	3 (60.0)	5(100.0)
30-35	34 (69.3)	--	15 (30.7)	49(100.0)

Characteristics	Not breastfeeding presently	Exclusively breastfeeding	Breastfeeding with other supplements	Total children
Age of child (in months) 36-41	3 (75.0)	--	1 (25.0)	4(100.0)
42-47	34(85.0)	--	6 (15.0)	40(100.0)
Sex of Child				
Males	40 (29.8)	50(37.3)	44(32.9)	134(100.0)
Females	51(58.6)	17(19.5)	19(21.9)	87(100.0)
Total	91 (41.2)	67(30.3)	63 (28.5)	**221(100.0)**

Table 6.9 : Percent distribution of duration (in months) of children breast fed by their mother

	Duration of breast feeding				
		Frequency	Percent	Valid Percent	Cumulative Percent
Valid	0-5 months	20	3.6	9.1	9.1
	6-11 months	40	7.2	18.2	27.3
	12-17 months	12	2.1	5.5	32.7
	18-23 months	50	8.9	22.7	55.5
	24-29 months	5	0.9	2.3	57.7
	30-35 months	49	8.8	22.3	80.0
	36-41 months	4	0.7	1.8	81.8
	42-47 months	40	7.2	18.2	100.0
	Total	221	39.4	100.0	

Figure 78 A Breastfed baby girl.

Duration of breast feeding

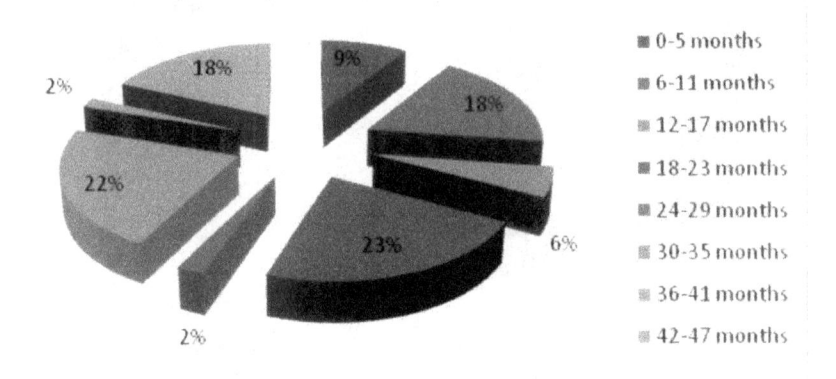

- 0-5 months: 9%
- 6-11 months: 18%
- 12-17 months: 6%
- 18-23 months: 23%
- 24-29 months: 2%
- 30-35 months: 22%
- 36-41 months: 2%
- 42-47 months: 18%

Figure 79 Graphical representation of duration children breast fed (in months)

It is found from the study that the proportion of children who are fully breastfed decreases rapidly with age as children are gradually weaned from the breast. Majority of women in the slums have stopped exclusive breastfeeding to their children by 24-29 months of age. Exclusive breastfeeding was thus influenced partially by the gender of child, education of the mother and overall health conditions of the child and mother as elucidated from the study.

Chapter 7

Determinants of fertility, infant mortality

Various socio-demographic factors affect the fertility of the slum women, their contraceptive usages and mortality of the infants born in the slums. So how fertility, infant mortality and birth control methods are related with these factors have been studied through quantitative analysis adopting certain statistical tests. In this chapter, these have been taken as hypotheses and has been tested through correlation and regression equation methods, using SPSS 21.0.

Fertility, infant mortality, and the acceptance of fertility control methods are influenced by a variety of interrelated factors such as age at marriage, education and economic status. Lower infant mortality coupled with higher fertility is a strong motivational factor in the acceptance of fertility control measures. As the relative effect of each factor differs from one population to another, it is of interest to study their association and their contribution (singular as well as collective) in the present population of slum dwellers.

Bio-social factors such as woman's age, educational level, and age at marriage, economic status and religious attitudes have an effect on fertility (RGI-Fertility Survey, 1971; Elamin and Bhuyan, 1999), in addition to, conception control practices and attitudes, (Bhuyan and Ahmed, 1984). Urbanization, in general, leads to modernization and more development, higher literacy, awareness about health care, more contraceptive use, a higher living standard and prevalence of nuclear families, and all these factors play a significant role in lowering fertility (UN, 1953; De Jong, 1972; NFHS 1998-99, 2002). However, in the slums of Kolkata these positive effects of urbanization were not significantly found. So the following three hypotheses have been conceptualized and statistically tested.

Null Hypothesis 1: *Fertility among women in slums in Kolkata is not affected by several factors*

Alternative Hypotheis1: *Fertility among women in slums in Kolkata is affected by several factors*

Numerous factors affect fertility, such as age of the woman at present, ideal no. of children, desired no. of sons, age at menarche, infant mortality, type of house, annual per capita income, woman's age at marriage, husband's education, use of birth control methods and woman's education. The relationship is statistically significant in all the cases except annual per capita income of the household. Age of woman at present, is the most important factor affecting fertility of these women. Number of live births per women increases as the age of woman increases. Age of the woman, ideal no. of children, desire no. of sons, age at menarche, infant mortality and type of house are responsible for increasing fertility (a positive correlation). Table 7.1 shows the linear regression equations for the factors that have a significant relationship with fertility.

Table 7.1 : Correlation results of Hypothesis 1

Correlations		
		Fertility among women in slums of Kolkata, affected by various factors
Fertility among women in slums of Kolkata, affected by various factors	Pearson Correlation	1
Age	Pearson Correlation	.642**
No. of children	Pearson Correlation	.566**
Desired gender of the child to be born	Pearson Correlation	.739**
Education	Pearson Correlation	.686**
Husbands' Education	Pearson Correlation	.686**
Age of menarche	Pearson Correlation	.580**
Usage of contraceptives	Pearson Correlation	-.475**
Number of Children living (or ever born)	Pearson Correlation	.442**
Monthly Income	Pearson Correlation	-.068
Type of house	Pearson Correlation	.637**
Age at 1st marriage	Pearson Correlation	.384**
**. Correlation is significant at the 0.01 level (2-tailed).		

Conversely, annual per capita income, woman's age at marriage, husband's education, use of birth control methods and woman's education have reducing effect on woman's fertility.

Educational status of females is the most important variable accounting for fertility decline (Coale, 1965; Ghosh, 1975; Zachariah, 1981; Jolly, 1981; Johnson, 1993). Among these, women fertility decreases as the educational level increases. In India, women with high school and above education have markedly lower average fertility than the less educated (Mandelbaum, 1974). Late age at marriage results in low fertility, as there is delay in exposure to the risk of conception (Agarwala, 1967; Durch, 1980; Nag, 1982; Pandey and Talwar, 1987; Yadav and Badari, 1997). The results of the present study also reflect that age at marriage has a direct bearing on fertility. Finding of other researchers also reflects that educational level, economic status, desired no. of sons, use of BCM, etc. affects fertility (RGI-fertility survey, 1971; Basu et al., 1988; Bhasin and Kshatriya, 1990; Elamin and Bhuyan, 1999; Bhasin and Nag, 2002).

Though the relationship with the economic status is non-significant, it is expected to influence fertility negatively (Table 22). It is generally agreed that fertility is negatively related to income (Stycos, 1968; Mahadevan, 1989) and especially, to female earnings (Becker, 1981; Schultz, 1985), though some studies have shown a positive relationship between economic status and fertility (Driver, 1963; Mandelbaum, 1974). The people of lower economic groups tend to have more children for the need of economic support. Also, women of poorer groups have tendency to bear more children because of higher infant mortality (and therefore these women have shorter lactation and anovulatory periods before becoming fecund again) and consequently need more children to replace the lost ones (Wyon and Gordon, 1971; Mahadevan, 1979).

Table 7.2: Model summary of different factors establishing alternative Hypothesis 1

Model Summary				
Model	R	R Square	Adjusted R Square	Std. Error of the Estimate
1	.765	.581	.580	.207
2	.244	.062	.061	.190
3	.213	.037	.035	.171
4	.211	.031	.030	.169
5	.190	.026	.025	.167
6	.188	.023	.022	.167
7	.180	.016	.015	.166

The equation regression of live births, (reflecting the fertility of women) was:

Predicted live births= -.475 × women's age 0.122 × ideal no. of children 0.457 × infant mortality 0.831 × women's education -0.034 × use of BCM -0.383 × women's age at marriage -0.064 × desired no. of sons + 0.242

The results of stepwise multiple regression analysis for fertility reflect that among fertility-related independent variables, woman's age, ideal no. of children, infant mortality, woman's education, use of birth control methods, woman's age at marriage and desire no. of sons show statistically significant association. Woman's age is the most important variable in determining the level of the fertility, followed by ideal no. of children and infant mortality. Among the slum dwelling woman's age could explain fifty eight percent of the variance in fertility. Additional, six percent of the variance can be explained by adding ideal no. of children. When infant mortality is added, 3.5 percent fertility is further explained.

Null Hypothesis 2: *There is no association of infant mortality with factors affecting it among children in Kolkata slum.*

Alternative Hypothesis 2: *There is association of infant mortality with factors affecting it among children in Kolkata slum.*

Among slum dwellers infant loss per woman, taken as indicator of infant mortality, is associated with a wide variety of bio-social factors such as woman's age, women's education, husband's education, type of house, woman's age at marriage and annual per capita income. Infant deaths results in more number of live births as women try to compensate their loss in order to achieve their desired number of surviving children. Generally, individuals use family planning methods only after achieving a desired number of children. Age of woman, number of live births per ever married women and type of house have positive effect on Infant mortality (Table 7.3). Woman who have higher infant mortality tend to have higher fertility and vice-a-versa, which is a well-established fact (Chen et al., 1974; Choudhury et al., 1976; Preston, 1978). This is also true for Slum dwellers understudy. Higher fertility could be a mechanism of compensation to achieve desired number of children.

Table 7.3: Correlation of Hypothesis 2

Correlations		
		There is Association of infant mortality with factors affecting it among children in Kolkata slum
There is Association of infant mortality with factors affecting it among children in Kolkata slum	Pearson Correlation	1
	Sig. (2-tailed)	
	N	559
Age	Pearson Correlation	.604**
	Sig. (2-tailed)	.000
	N	559
Education	Pearson Correlation	.697**
	Sig. (2-tailed)	.000
	N	559
Husbands' Education	Pearson Correlation	.697**
	Sig. (2-tailed)	.000
	N	559
Number of Children living (or ever born)	Pearson Correlation	.428**
	Sig. (2-tailed)	.000
	N	559
Monthly Income	Pearson Correlation	-.076
	Sig. (2-tailed)	.072
	N	559
Age at 1st marriage	Pearson Correlation	.377**
	Sig. (2-tailed)	.000
	N	559
Type of house	Pearson Correlation	.609**
	Sig. (2-tailed)	.000
	N	559
**. Correlation is significant at the 0.01 level (2-tailed).		

Women's education, husband's education, women's age at marriage and annual per capita income has a negative effect on infant mortality. Increase in educational level of husband and wife decreases the chances of infant mortality as educated parents have greater awareness about general sanitation, hygiene, nutrition and availability and usage of health services. Educated mother ensure lower infant mortality by providing adequate care to their infants in terms of hygiene and health services (Caldwell, 1979; Nag, 1983; Bhasin and Kshatriya, 1990; UN, 1994). Barring few irregularities it is generally agreed that paternal education also have a negative effect on infant mortality (Caldwell, 1979; Nag, 1983; Hobcraft et al., 1984; UN, 1985; Mahadevan, 1989; Chachra and Bhasin, 1998; Bhasin and Nag, 2002). However, lower child mortality is noticed only beyond primary level of education. Women who marry young tend to have children at a younger age. As they are not physiologically mature, this leads to higher infant mortality. Among Slum dwellers income has a negative effect on infant mortality.

Table 7.4: Model summary of factors establishing alternative Hypothesis 2

Model Summary					
Model	R	R Square	Adjusted R Square	Std. Error of the Estimate
1	.215	.021	.020	.209
2	.284	.091	.090	.198
3	.753	.567	.564	.192
4	.761	.579	.576	.189
5	.763	.583	.579	.189

The equation regression of infant mortality was:

Predicted infant mortality= 0.183 × live births 0.105 × women's age -0.012

Low-income group households have lesser resources to combat illness and environmental hazards resulting in higher infant mortality (Model 5). This association is well documented (Jain, 1985; UN, 1985; DasGupta, 1990), though not always monotonic. Live births (Model 4) and woman's age are found to be statistically significant. Fertility is the most important variable in determining the level of the infant mortality (Model 2), followed by woman's age (Model 1). About nine percent of the variance in infant mortality could be explained by fertility of the woman. Woman's age could explain around two percent of the variation in infant mortality.

Null Hypothesis 3: *There is no association between use of birth control methods (BCM) and factors affecting it among women in Kolkata slums.*

Alternative Hypothesis 3: *There is association between use of birth control methods (BCM) and factors affecting it among women in Kolkata slums.*

Factors like son preference, women's age, literacy, number of living children and number of living sons influence contraceptive use (Gandotra and Das, 1990; Levine et al., 1992; Bora and Jha, 2001). Couples with fewer sons are more likely to continue having more children, besides, have shorter birth intervals and are also less probable to use contraception (Das Gupta, 1987; Nag, 1991; Raju and Bhat, 1995). Among the Kolkata slum dwellers usage of family planning methods is associated with a number of factors such as woman's age, woman's education, and woman's age at marriage, ideal number of children and surviving no. of children. Usage of family planning methods increases with the education of the woman, woman's age at marriage and education of the husband (Table 7.5). Thus, education of women and that of her husband plays an important role in the adoption of family planning methods. Higher educated women have a better knowledge to use non-terminal method more effectively (Bumpass, 1987). Acceptance of female sterilization, which is a terminal birth control method, is influenced by the number of living children in addition to the number of sons and is usually accepted when the couples are sure that they have completed with their family size and gender preference (Khan, 1980; Rajaram, 1998, Das and Acharya, 1999; Rajaretnam, 2000).

Table 7.5: Correlation of Hypothesis 3

Correlations		
		There is association of use of birth control methods (BCM) and factors affecting it among women in Kolkata slums
There is association of use of birth control methods (BCM) and factors affecting it among women in Kolkata slums	Pearson Correlation	1
	Sig. (2-tailed)	
	N	559
Age	Pearson Correlation	.674**
	Sig. (2-tailed)	.000
Education	Pearson Correlation	.678**
	Sig. (2-tailed)	.000
	N	559
Husbands' Education	Pearson Correlation	.678**
	Sig. (2-tailed)	.000
	N	559
Number of Children living (or ever born)	Pearson Correlation	.464**
	Sig. (2-tailed)	.000
	N	559
Monthly Income	Pearson Correlation	-.082
	Sig. (2-tailed)	.054
	N	559
Age at 1st marriage	Pearson Correlation	.397**

	Sig. (2-tailed)	.000
	N	559
Type of house	Pearson Correlation	.676**
	Sig. (2-tailed)	.000
	N	559
No. of children	Pearson Correlation	.588**
	Sig. (2-tailed)	.000
	N	559
Desired gender of the child to be born	Pearson Correlation	.808**
	Sig. (2-tailed)	.000
	N	559
**. Correlation is significant at the 0.01 level (2-tailed).		

Among slum dwellers female sterilization or/and ligation is one of the popular birth control method, and it is expected that family size and gender preference plays a role in acceptance of female sterilization. Usage of family planning methods decreases with woman's age, desired no. of sons and annual per capita income. Association of use of BCM with variables namely woman's age, surviving no. of children, woman's education, woman's age at marriage, and ideal no. of children is statistically significant. Among women who are younger and have lesser number of children appear to be more willing to use contraception as compared to women who are older and have more children. Couples at a higher income level are more likely to use contraceptives.

Table 7.6: Model summary of different factors establishing alternative Hypothesis 3

Model Summary				
Model	R	R Square	Adjusted R Square	Std. Error of the Estimate
1	.157	.003	.002	.194
2	.175	.011	.009	.190
3	.186	.023	.022	.184
4	.218	.046	.045	.183
5	.227	.062	.060	.182
6	.346	.172	.170	.181

The equation regression of usage of BCM among women dwelling in slum:

Predicted use of BCM= 1.634 × women's age -0.017 × surviving no. of children-0.073 × ideal no. of children 0.126

Stepwise multivariate regression analysis reflects that the association of usage of family planning methods with woman's age, surviving number of children and ideal number of children is statistically significant. The most important variable in determining the level of use of birth control methods among slum dwellers is woman's age followed by surviving no. of children and ideal number of children. About 17 percent of the variance in use of BCM (Model 6) could be explained by woman's age. Addition of surviving no. of children and ideal number of children contribute for smaller proportion of variance (Model 4 and 5, respectively).

Hence, after analyzing the different parameters related to the livelihood of the slum dwellers, especially women, the following insights can be gathered from the conditions prevailing around their health, social and cultural practices, fertility, and perception to different causes existing around them and about their child's health.

1. Economic conditions: Irregular employment, poor access to fair credit

2. Social conditions: Widespread alcoholism, gender inequity, poor educational status

3. Living environment: Poor access to safe water supply and sanitation facilities, overcrowding, poor housing and insecure land tenure

4. Access and use of public health care services: Lack of access to ICDS and primary health care services, poor quality of health care

5. Health and disease: High prevalence of diarrhea, fever and cough among children

6. Negotiating capacity: Lack of organized community collective efforts in slums among slum dwellers

Thus, it is seen that higher fertility is associated with older women, which increases with the addition of higher ideal no of children and if the infant mortality is higher. In case of infant mortality, it is expected that if infant mortality is lowered then it may facilitate fertility reduction. Acceptance and use of family planning methods among older women is lower, during their active reproductive period they were less aware and less receptive for family planning. The likelihood for usage of birth control methods increases with the increase in surviving children, however, it further declines if the women have higher desire for sons. Fertility, infant mortality and use of birth control methods, thus, influence each other.

Chapter 8

Summary and observations

The urban population of India is one of the largest in the world at 377.1 million. The pace of urbanization far exceeds the rate at which basic infrastructure and services can be provided. Consequently one third of them are in a state of chronic poverty, living in the slums. In this way slum has become an integral part of the entire urban community and the poor population constitute a significant proportion of urban population. The slum population is constantly increasing and it has doubled in the past two decades. India's slum-dwelling population rose from 27.9 million in 1981 to over 40 million in 2001 and 93.06 million in 2011 as per Census of India 2011. One in six urban Indians and every eighth urban children in India in the age-group of 0 - 6 years lives in slums. About 7.6 million Indian children are living in this degrading urban environment with the burden of diseases. They live in cramped, poorly ventilated houses and in most cases, they are unclean and unfit for human habitation. This is clearly reflected in their health conditions. Both the water-borne diseases like diarrhoea and air-borne diseases like acute respiratory infections are very common among these children.

The slums of Kolkata can be divided into three groups: the older ones, up to 150 years' old, in the heart of the city, are associated with early urbanization. The second group dates from the 1940s and 1950s and emerged as an outcome of industrialization-based rural/urban migration, locating themselves around industrial sites and near infra-structural arteries. The third group came into being after the independence of India and took vacant urban lands and areas along roads, canals and on marginal lands.

In Kolkata 1.5 million people, or one third of the population live in the slums, in overcrowded and unsanitary conditions without adequate basic amenities. Neither religion, or language, nor caste can be shown to have a strong influence on the physical structure of slums as the population share equal socioeconomic deprivation. The slum dwellers suffer from living in poorly ventilated housing, lack of sanitation, shared toilets, low income, and burden of disease coupled with malnutrition and ill health. The deteriorating urban environment, the lack of safe drinking water and poor nutritional status influence the burden of disease and health outcomes. The health indicators for women and children reveal that they are considerably worse off. Women's unequal status in social, economic and political life in general has made them the most vulnerable section of the society. Factors such as poverty, overwork and social inequality accounted for considerable neglect of their own health. The demands of managing a house, taking care of the husband and children, and going out to work to bring in extra money tends to place the women's own health quite low on the list of priorities .It may be often seen that unless they have more than one complaint of ill health they do not seek treatment. About one-third of the total disease burden among women aged 15 to 49 years is linked to health problems arising out of pregnancy, childbirth, abortion and reproductive tract infections.

Ever-married women aged 15-49 years and their children aged 0-4 years were chosen from a sample of 559 households from four randomly selected slums of Kolkata. Data were collected by fieldwork through frequent visits to the studied areas by single investigator, on the followings : demography, housing and household characteristics, marital status, educational and occupational status, reproductive performances of women including fertility, morbidity, menarcheal and menopausal age, common aliment symptoms, activity pattern, health maintenance, child birth and antenatal care, delivery and postnatal care, immunization, child health and morbidity, diseases and treatment, feeding practices and supplementation methods prevalent among the studied population. Raw data was transformed into simple percentage form for lucid presentation and easy understanding of the facts that lies in the study area and population. The facts derived from analyses were also presented with pictorial method for visual interpretation and photographic technique has also been adopted for depiction of the ground realities of slums.

The age sex structure of the slum population shows a large share of the total population is below 15 years of age, while the concentration of the population between 15 to 34 years is also very high and only a meagre percentage of population survives upto old age. The median age of the slum population is 19.2 years, indicating a young (growing) population. The sex ratio in the studied slums is found to be 960 which is more or less similar to the state sex ratio of 950. Moreover, it was found that though in the age groups 0 to 4 years males outnumbered females, there are female preponderances over the males in some of the age groups between 30-49 years, in the studied slums. The population pyramid reveals that the slum population has a very high birth rate as well as a very high death rate.

The marital status of the studied population (i.e. the women between 15-49 years of age groups) revealed that about 4% of the married females are below 18 years, which is the legal age of marriage, indicating a tendency of child marriage among the girls of lower socio-economic groups. Most of the married population (80%) is between the ages of 20-39 years, while nearly 14% of the female population is deserted and widowed. It has been observed through case studies that in most cases these separated women become the head of the household consisting of her children.

The educational status of the studied group reveals that majority of the slum women are illiterate (55.6%) though 44.90% of them possessing the ability to sign their own name without the ability to read and write. Most of the literates possess only primary education, and majority of the younger generation having secondary level education and a very negligible percentage of them having qualifications of higher secondary and graduation level. The probable causes behind such poor educational standard can be attributed to early marriage, lack of motivation and lack of opportunities as the females are often forced to take up odd jobs at an early age for supporting their families financially.

The slum women mostly engage themselves as household maids, cooks, ayahs or attendants, vegetable or fish vendors. Some of them are also doing petty businesses and others are engaged as tailors, clerks or peons. Majority of them are working as household maids or "kajerloks" (in Bengali) as part-time domestic maids, in employer's house. The average monthly incomes of the respondents are between Rs 1500 to Rs 5000 per month. Their working hours varies mostly between 10 to 12 hours a day. As the women are employed in different types of work outside the slums, the travelling time is mostly less than half an hour, walking distance. Besides walking, some of them also cycled and few commute by bus or auto-rickshaws to their workplaces.

Reproductive health of these slum women has been determined in the present study .The mean menarcheal age is found to be 13.9 years which is almost same as that for lower socio-economic urban Indian, whereas the median age at first marriage for women aged 15-49 years in the slums is 17 years (mean 17.05 years), which is just below the legal permissible age. The onset and cessation of childbearing are important indicators of fertility. In the studied slums, early births are common for ever-married women .The median age at first birth is marginally higher for younger women than the older women.

Overall, the median age at first birth is 19 years (mean 19.59 years) for women aged 15-49 years indicating relatively early marriage and childbearing. The childbearing was completed by 30 years of age, for more than half women in age group 45-49 years, with 29 years as median age at last childbirth. No one reported having a birth after age of 39 years indicating that generally childbearing is complete by this age.

The ever-married slum women in the childbearing years have borne an average of 3.34 children and have 3.10 currently living which means, for over three children born around ninety percent is surviving, indicating some reproductive loss in form of still births and abortions. The mean number of children ever born increases steadily with age, reaching a high of over five children per woman for the 45-49 age groups.

Majority of the women included in this study (nearly 70 percent) said that they are suffering from some kind of reproductive health problems such as hemorrhoids, fistula, prolapse, urinary tract infection, vaginal discharges and menstrual disorders.

They reported current symptoms suggestive of at least one type of gynecological morbidity. Anemia (28 percent) and lower reproductive tract infections (17 percent) were commonly reported, while menstrual problems were also reported by 9.8 percent. Symptoms associated with acute pelvic inflammatory disease (4.6 percent) and urinary tract infections (3.5 percent) were less common. All other symptom categories were reported infrequently: hemorrhoids (2.5 percent), prolapse (2.1 percent) and fistula (1.6 percent). Most of the symptoms of the reproductive morbidity among the studied population lasted between less than three months to one year. However a large proportion of these women, ranging from 20 percent to about 50 percent, reported their symptoms to have lasted for more than one year. The mean durations ranged between 12 months for symptoms associated with prolapse and 26 months for white/colored vaginal discharge whereas the problems of anemia and lower reproductive tract infections persisted for longer time-periods.

Health status of women has been mainly discussed through the methods and practices of family planning among currently married women, ante-natal and post natal care, place of delivery along with awareness in mothers regarding AIDS, contraception, immunization and breastfeeding.

Among the slum dwellers it has been observed that despite having knowledge about family planning and the various means of birth-control, very meager amount is interested and use means of contraception (34%) and majority (66%) does not adhere to such usage. Among those who use contraceptives, majority opt for oral contraceptive pills (16% out of 34%), followed by condoms (8%) and traditional methods (7%) such as, abstinence, safe period, lactational amenorrhea. Rest of the population, who do not adopt birth control measures have reasons such as, desires for more children and desire for son if the previous child is a daughter. The other factors were lack of motivation (19%), health factors (5%) or lack of knowledge. Antenatal Care (ANC) is a crucial aspect of maternal health; about 75 percent of the mothers have received antenatal check-ups in the slums. For those who did not receive ANC, 71.5 percent felt that it is unnecessary unless there is a complication. For 12.5 percent woman, check-ups are costly. And 8.9 percent mothers said that their families did not allow them to get antenatal check-ups or they did not have time to go for antenatal check-ups. This indicates that there are substantial population who need to be aware about the availability and benefits of these reproductive health services in the slums. Regarding the place of delivery, majority of child-births in the slums have took place in their own home while over one-fourth have took place in health facilities. Out of the births in health facilities, only small proportion has taken place in private medical institutions (0.9 per cent) and 26.2 per cent in public health facilities. Institutional deliveries are more common for births to mother aged 15 -34 years than for mothers aged 35+. They are also more common for first births than for later births. From the detailed study it can be said that the likelihood of institutional delivery increases with mother's educational level indicating that awareness about the benefits of professional medical care during pregnancy and delivery is more among the women with higher education.

It was found from the interviews that majority of the slum dwelling women continued with their job, without taking any leaves during the pregnancy period. Due to their poor economic conditions and temporary nature of work, most of them fear losing job if they take leave for long duration. Leaves were taken during one month prior to delivery and only for two- three months post-delivery. Mostly it had been observed that those women engaged as household-maids had a normal delivery.

A look at the treatment pattern for common ailments among the women in the slums reflects that majority of them resorted to alternative methods of medical treatments like homeopathy, ayurveda, naturopathy and faith healing. They have been adopting various indigenous methods to treat themselves mostly in their daily lives. 70% of the women had awareness regarding AIDS and its prevention. Most of the mothers were also aware about child immunization.

Regarding the health of the slum children, it was observed that majority (97.9 %) were administered the polio vaccine, 78% were given DPT and 80% BCG. Measles immunization was relatively lesser among the studied population. Among those who did not immunize their children against these diseases, claimed that the children do not need the vaccination; others answered that they had lesser access to a medical facility; while others said the cost of giving vaccine caused hindrance.

Among the childhood aliments, affecting the infants and children in slums, diarrhea was the most common, followed by acute respiratory infections (ARI), and influenza. One in every fifteen children under four years of age suffered from the acute respiratory infection ,cough accompanied by short and fast breathing, at some time during the two weeks before the study .The most vulnerable for air-borne diseases were children between 0-5 months of age. Negligible differences are observed according to the gender of the child. The prevalence of respiratory diseases varies rather irregularly by mother's educational level. Fever is another major cause of child morbidity, which accompanies various illnesses importantly with malaria. The incidence of fever, during two weeks was lower than diarrhoea. About twelve percent of the children suffered from fever. Children aged 6-23 months were somewhat more prone to fever. Fever is also more common in females than males. No consistent relationship is observed between the prevalence of fever and the education of the mother.

Diarrhoea is the most common of the three conditions examined during the study. One-fifth of the children under four years of age had diarrhea during two weeks prior to. The incidence of diarrhoea declines with increasing age. Children aged 36-47 months are least susceptible to diarrhoea. Diarrhoea is more prevalent among males than females and higher among children of illiterate women.

A look at the treatment pattern reflects that majority of children who suffered from Acute Respiratory Infection were taken to a health facility (e.g. hospital) or provider (doctor) for treatment .About 14 percent of the children with ARI did not receive any treatment. Suffering children were most often treated with pills and cough syrup. More than four-fifth of the children with fever was taken to a health facility or provider for treatment .Majority of children were treated with pills and injections. Anti-malarial medication was give to less than ten percent of the children. Treatment at a health facility or by a health provider was more common for children under two years of age and for male children. The differentials in the likelihood of taking treatment or medical advice for diarrhoea with respect to mother's education do not reflect a consistent pattern. It was observed that the likelihood of taking the child to the hospital increases with increase in the level of education of the mother; however, less than sixteen percent of the children having diarrhoea were treated at home.

It was found that the majority of the mothers were aware of the fact that it is inappropriate to reduce the frequency of breastfeeding or total intake of mother's milk or other fluids when a child is suffering with diarrhoea. In most of the children the amount of other fluids given was maintained at the same frequency although one in every six children with diarrhoea was given less fluid than they received before the diarrhoea began. The percentage of children who were given fewer fluids was less among those who were under one year than those who were older. For majority of children the frequency of breastfeeding was also unchanged. The frequency increased during the diarrhoea in over one-sixth of children and decreased in less than ten percent of children. The frequency of breastfeeding was the same for a larger proportion of children under one year than those who were older.

Breastfeeding practices have significant effects on child survival and health as well as maternal fertility and maternal health. The respondents were aware of the Reproductive and Child Health programme of the Government of India which recommends that infants should be exclusively breastfed up to six months of age and continued as long as possible for the mother. All of the children aged 0-5 months were found to be fully breastfed while 92.5 percent of the children below one year were breastfed exclusively, remaining were partially breastfed (i.e., received supplements such as other milk like cow's milk, other liquid, or solid or mushy food). The proportion of children who are fully breastfed decreased with age as children are gradually weaned from the breast. Majority of children in the KMC slums have stopped exclusive breastfeeding by 24-29 months of age. Exclusive breastfeeding was influenced partially by the gender of child, education of the mother and overall health conditions of the child and mother as elucidated from the study.

Thus from the findings, it could be pointed out that the huge burden of diseases that affects the slum population is mostly due to lack of sanitation, lack of ventilation, lack of education, and lack of awareness. Very recently the Indian Government promised to prioritize the healthcare of these masses and implement a universal medical insurance. Till the end of 2013-14 total expenditure on general health in India was a meager 4 percent of the gross domestic product. The slum populations, whose minimum health expenditure should ideally have been covered by the state, are left with no recourse but to turn to private hospitals for treatment. Most of them cannot afford that. The result is further impoverishment of the poor; or debilitation and death owing to lack of treatment.

Finally, it is to be mentioned that the transition from an agrarian to urban India necessitates a reorientation of the national polices and priorities. Urban slums are mostly deprived human settlements, which are demographically, socially, economically and environmentally vulnerable. It must be realized that the average figures of urban areas hide the stark reality of the deprived population in slums. Clear cut data on slum population is not available easily. The health problems of the urban poor are related to a complex web of causation. The provision of 'Primary Health Care' therefore has to be provided as a part of overall comprehensive urban slum development. "Primary health care" (PHC) includes promotion of proper nutrition and an adequate supply of safe water; basic sanitation; maternal and child care, including family planning; immunization against the major infectious diseases; prevention and control of locally endemic diseases; education concerning prevailing health problems and the methods of preventing and controlling them; and appropriate treatment for common diseases and injuries. India's commitment to provide Primary Health Care (PHC) to the masses dates back to the recommendations of the Bhore Committee in 1946. India's rededication to the PHC approach in 1978, implicit in the signing of the Alma Ata declaration of "Health for All", 2000 AD, redefined this approach for provision of health care to the masses. The concept of Public-Private Partnership (PPP) has been popular in the last decade of the last millennium and has now become an increasingly popular option in health care delivery system in India. Historically many such projects have been implemented in different states of India like Karnataka, Tamil Nadu, Rajasthan, and Gujarat. Partnership with the private sector is particularly critical in the Indian context. Governments in India presuppose that partnerships could help in ameliorating the problem of poor health services delivery at two levels: a) to improve delivery mechanisms and, b) to increase mobilization of resources for healthcare. Other presumed benefits of partnerships include improvement in quality of services, reduced cost of care either due to competition or through economies of scale, re directing the public resources to other areas, reduction in duplication of services, adoption of best practices, targeted services to the poor, and improve self regulation and accountability. However it is clear that, the government is ultimately responsible for the delivery of services. If there are any deficiencies from the private sector the responsibility for dereliction of services fall on the government health functionaries. In almost all partnerships, the principal public partner is the department of health and family welfare, either state or central, directly or through health facility level committees. The private sector represented in the form of individual physicians, commercial contractors, large private and corporate super-specialty hospitals and NGOs. Some of the partnerships deal with simple contracts (diet, laundry, cleaning, etc) while others are more complex involving many stakeholders. Most of the projects are specific to a geographical region while some benefit an entire state. In West Bengal, the state level policy on public-private partnership was framed after launching few pilot projects. In terms of the monetary value, the least valued contract was in providing dietary services at a rate of Rs. 27 per meal for about 30 patients per day, in Bhagajatin Hospital, in Kolkata. However, there are not many reports on Public-Private-Partnership in Primary Health Care services in slums of Kolkata.

In sum, it can be pointed out that in India deficiencies of the public health system could be overcome by reforms in the health sector. One of the important reform strategies is collaborating with the private sector in the form of Public-Private Partnership. Due to the deficiencies in the public sector health systems, the urban poor in India are forced to seek services from the private sector, under immense economic duress. In the health sector, the Public-Private-Partnership as a social entity pools the best features of the two merging authorities of government and private sectors. Therefore, further studies should be oriented in exploring this to the fullest extent to promote health of the urban poor population in our country.

From the study it can easily be said that improved housing condition along with physical infrastructure facilities and civic amenities like water supply, sanitation, latrine, drainage, and proper garbage disposal must be integrated for enhancing the quality of life and improved health conditions. Both National and State Governments have to take various developmental plans. Some plans which have already been taken for urban development, such as Jawaharlal Nehru National Urban Renewal Mission (JNNURM), Basic Services to the Urban Poor (BSUP), the National Slum Development Programme, 1996-2006 (NSDP), Valmiki Ambedkar Awas Yojana, 2001-2006 (VAMBAY) should be implemented with full effect in the slums.

Though about a decade ago the Slum Upgrading Facility (SUF) had been activated with the help from British Overseas Bank and Asian Development Bank for upgradation projects in Kolkata, for the rehabilitation of slum dwellers but most of the works still remains unaccomplished. Some development may be noticed in electricity connections and tap-water supply but overall improvement in the health sectors of the Kolkata slums is yet to be achieved. Prompt attention is required for the eradication of extreme poverty and hunger, to achieve universal primary education, promote gender equality and empower women, reduce child mortality, improve maternal health, combat AIDS, malaria and other diseases, ensuring environmental sustainability.

CPSIA information can be obtained
at www.ICGtesting.com
Printed in the USA
BVHW040226170423
662367BV00003B/560